PROVEN SKILLS
LEADERSHIP, AN

TAKING CHARGE
of Your
Time & Stress

DR. LLOYD ELDER

SKILLTRACK®
L E A D E R S H I P
A SkillTrack® Leadership Publication

salt light
PUBLISHING
A Division of Publishers Solution

TAKING CHARGE
of Your
Time & Stress

By Dr. Lloyd Elder
©2013 Lloyd Elder and Associates, Inc.. All rights reserved.

ISBN: 978-1-937925-11-6

Published By:

A Division of Publishers Solution

14805 Forest Rd., Ste 205 • Forest, VA 24551
www.PublishersSolution.com

Published With:

A SkillTrack® Leadership Publication

Cover & Interior Design by:
Heather Kirk, GraphicsForSuccess.com

BOOK TOPICS: 1. RELIGION / Christian Life / Personal Growth;
2. SELF-HELP / Time Management; 3. SELF-HELP / Stress Management

TABLE OF CONTENTS

PART 1
Taking Charge of Your Time: "Having the Time of Your Life"

Objective: *To explore the principles, practices, and benefits of time management, as in fact, life management, and to make application to leadership and ministry.*

Table of Contents

TAKING CHARGE of Your *Time & Stress*

PART 2
Taking Charge of Your Stress: "For the Sake of Life and Ministry"

Objective: *To advance proven skills for managing stress in Christian ministry and everyday living: (1) by exploring ways to understand stress and its causes; (2) by examining practices to guard against excessive stress and burnout in church life and ministry; and (3) by developing proven strategies for life-long coping with stress.*

"Sharpen the Saw is the unique endowment of continuous improvement or self-renewal to overcome entropy."
Stephen R. Covey, *Principle-Centered Leadership*, p. 47

PREFACE AND ACKNOWLEDGEMENTS

On this page, let me share with you the "Why?" and "Who?" of this book. No one has more reason to be grateful than do I as a family member, a fellow believer, an educator, and a pastor. For more than two decades it has been my primary task to be a participant with others in the great enterprise to provide leadership development materials and opportunities to pastors and church ministry teams. This book is for you.

As an integral part of that, I am passionately committed to the usefulness of this book. In my own rather extensive and continuing contact with churches and ministers, I have learned from them that they have both needs and the aspirations to make improvement in these areas of practical ministry skills. I applaud those out there who are actually doing the work of the kingdom and wanting to be learning and developing servants.

My acknowledgements and gratitude are focused primarily on years of development leading to this publication project:

- To the churches through the years that both patiently taught me and let me put into practice some of these lessons; I was often a flawed, but a willing student.

- To Belmont University who allowed me the privilege and faculty task to establish the Moench Center for Church Leadership, the core of my work as an educator.

- To the ministry students in my classes at Belmont University, who seemed to learn about time and stress, although it was well before they knew how badly it would be needed.

- To other educational institutions and state organizations who called upon us for consultation, instruction, and leadership curriculum.

- To pastors, ministers, lay leaders, and conferees, already "in the trenches," who listened and discussed, and learned from each other and perhaps, from the guy at the front.

- To literally thousands who have purchased SkillTrack® Leadership publications and responded to us with encouragement, insights, and suggestions for the work of leadership skill development.

- To the Bivocational and Small Church Leadership Network (BSCLN) which has been such a constant partner in membership, administration, and leadership training of ministers.

- To Mr. and Mrs. Joe Brunson of Winnsboro TX, who have become partners in the national ministry of BSCLN and its Scholarship Project for leadership training opportunities.

- And last and the most, to Joyce M. Byrd, who has been a colleague in the Moench Center and full partner in all that we do through SkillTrack® Leadership and our Website: ServantLeadersToday.com.

- Joyce and Lloyd both express our deepest appreciation for Bill James and Heather Kirk for their outstanding publication services.

Let us all go on "taking charge of our lives and ministries" until the end of our days!

DEDICATION
To the Bivocational and Small Church Leadership Network

"Silent Champions, Doing Whatever It Takes"

"Champions are made inches at a time, by the whole team—on the practice field and in the game."
(From a team sports analogy)

Dedication to a Network? Yes, because of its kingdom mission: *"The mission of the Network is to encourage, promote and serve bivocational and smaller membership churches, ministers and their families as they do whatever it takes in Christ's kingdom serving within local congregations, communities, and to the ends of the world."* I have been proud to know and work beside a roll call of such champions in the Bivocational and Small Church Leadership Network.

Silent Champions? Yes, because these ministers have been called, and choose to serve, largely behind the headlines, often not even in the "back-story." Some of us have often said that ministers in the smaller churches are the backbone of today's Christian labor force, even that they are at the forefront facing the looming challenges ahead. Like the Apostle Paul, they may hold down two (or more) jobs, start new churches, serve mostly with lay volunteers, and desperately need to **"manage time and stress."** Yet, unlike the biblical champions, Paul and Barnabas, they may remain as unknown and silent as were Tychicus or Epaphroditus.

Who then are these silent champions? Adapting a classical definition: "These are they who have, through Christ alone, won the victory over their adversaries; who hold high the banner of the cross; who strive to enter, endure, and win in the long race of life; who live as worthy examples of our most holy faith; who serve in the company of other kingdom citizens; and who champion the biblical and contemporary cause of bivocational and smaller membership churches everywhere in the service of Christ." This book salutes you! Keep on running **"like a champion rejoicing to run his course." Ps. 19:5**

**Also, this Book is Dedicated to My Friends of a Lifetime
Joe and Joyce Brunson, of Winnsboro, Texas—
And in loving memory of Joyce Brunson, who died in October of a sudden illness.**

In September of 2012, Joe and Joyce made a partnership gift in support of the Bivocational and Small Church Leadership Network and its BSCLN Scholarship Project. Before Joyce's death, Joe had discussed their support for the BSCLN/SkillTrack® CD-ROM Leadership courses of study. Joe agreed that Skilltrack® book publications should be added to the Scholarship. With sincere thanks, this is that book.

INTRODUCTION

Journey, a proven concept of life and ministry: "Taking Charge of Your Time and Stress" is a spiritual journey filled with excitement and challenge: to take charge of your own life, leadership, and ministry. That is worthy of your very best each day of your life, and for the rest of your journey. On the other hand, remember:

> *"If you don't take charge of your life, others will be glad to do it*
> *for you, and you may not like the outcome."*

Since this is your journey, "no one can walk it for you" or tell you exactly how it ought to be done. The most others can do is to travel their faith-journey alongside you, seeking to obey Holy Scripture, to learn from their own experiences, to search resources for proven skills and best practices, and to enjoy thoroughly the benefits along the way. Actually, we may also be encouraged to record and apply these time and stress findings to life, family, leadership, and ministry. That is what this book intends to do—to lay down some markers along the way for fellow travelers on their journey.

A timely prayer for you: If at the outset I were to offer a prayer for you, and for myself, it would be one often prayed in languages throughout the world. The full text of this prayer was originally penned around 1940 for a sermon by German theologian, Reinhold Niebuhr:

> ***THE SERENITY PRAYER:*** *"God grant me the serenity to accept*
> *the things I cannot change; courage to change the things I can;*
> *and wisdom to know the difference."*

TAKING CHARGE of Your *Time & Stress*

What are the outcomes we hope for you in "taking charge of your time and stress?" What are the proven skills and best practices of taking charge of your life; and what are the resulting benefits from your intentional, disciplined experience with time and stress? These outcomes are packed into the course of study, in decisions and actions, both large and small:

- Accepting responsibility, accountability, and consequences of your actions
- Listening for the voice of God in your life; becoming more reflective and responsive
- Living a whole and balanced life; developing as a healthy autonomous person
- Taking charge of your life with purpose, significance, and satisfaction
- Keeping your family in the big picture, as an essential part of the whole of life
- Transforming your external landscape, avoiding the urge to take control of others
- Improving your ministry competence, performance, and productivity
- Making the most of new opportunities or staying put in your ministry, with satisfaction
- Caring for your spiritual, mental, social, and physical health

What about time and stress in one book? The book grows out of my journey. Through the years I have lectured and taught leadership courses to students and ministers from across the nation, often using my research and experience in the areas of time and stress management. These two topics have been applauded as helpful and relevant to both personal life and professional ministry. It has been most demanding and lots of fun! I have learned so much from these students and ministers, including that these two components of life are most vital to healthy personal life and productive leadership in ministry. So, this one book was developed to treat these as twin skill-sets and let each reader make the personal focus and application.

Part 1—Taking Charge of Your Time: *Having the Time of Your Life*

Part 2—Taking Charge of Your Stress: *For the Sake of Life and Ministry*

Each part has its own structure, objective, and unique contribution. For me, **time and stress are like twins in the same family. They both belong in the same family, but each needs to be treated appropriately.** The volume intends to be a practical theology text/workbook. You will find that the Parts have a kindred approach to development:

- Situation and audience: for pastors, other staff ministers, and lay leadership teams
- Biblical study and its application to life and leadership
- Living and learning lessons about time and stress, some of it the hard way
- Research into proven skills and best practices, in time and stress management
- Lessons learned from the experiences of others in active pastoral ministries
- Practical application to roles, relationships, and specific ministries
- Calls for reflection, analysis, inventory, and action: this is about your journey

Book Thesis and Process: Taking Charge of Your Time and Stress

- "Taking charge of your life" is one of the most exciting and challenging tasks you face each day, and for the rest of your life.
- "Taking charge" means that you accept responsibility, accountability, and actions for your life, as you seek to pursue purpose, significance, and balance.
- Time and stress are powerful and constant twin-components of your whole life: personal, family, leadership, and ministry.
- "Taking charge of your time and stress" is a daily frontline action in taking charge of your whole life. Start there and go on to pursue your largest dreams.
- Since you are the only one that can do it, this book offers you a resource of more than 150 proven skills and best practices as you journey forward.

The expanded **Table of Contents** contributes to the introduction of the book and each of its two parts. It also assists in the need to cross reference specific skills and practices. It is, in fact, intended to be a topical index for the whole book, not alphabetically arranged but ordered inside the context of the "taking charge" thesis. The **Annotated Bibliography** offers extensive resources, both in print and Websites, for the study of time and stress, but also to biblical studies, leadership and management. It includes the full information of works cited throughout the volume.

PART 1

TAKING CHARGE OF YOUR TIME:
"Having the Time of Your Life"

CHAPTER 1
Taking Charge Overview: Having the Time of Your Life

KEY TEXT—Ephesians 5:15-16

Be very careful, then, how you live [walk]—not as unwise but as wise, making the most of every opportunity [time], because the days are evil. **(NIV)**

A Personal Perspective

Over the years the content of this book has been hammered out and put into several sizes and shapes, including research notes, conferences messages, lectures, study guides, and classroom syllabi. Only now has it been published in book format and placed as one of two bookends for the minister's life: **taking charge of your time and stress.** As we will often claim, "time management is really life management."

A word from a ministers' conference: Several years ago I used this research as a study guide in a ministers' conference in my neighboring state of Mississippi. I had been "waxing eloquent" on the subject of having the time of your life and enjoying lively discussion from those in the session. (I seem to learn more about what I am teaching if I also take time to listen up.) During an afternoon break, one of the pastors, beginning to show some silver hair around the temples, asked the question, "Dr. Elder, where were you 20 years ago when I first began to pastor?"

That pastor's question has stayed around me whether in the classroom, behind the lectern, or at my writing desk— as well as my own practice of Christian ministry.

During that same kind of leadership training conference, I have asked ministers to make their current "time-bind" list. Then to walk around and visit with one to others, edit their lists, and then let's sit down and talk about it. Beyond the boundaries of these pages, you may want to be up-front with yourself and list five or so high priorities that call out to you to take charge of your time and get on with it.

"Taking Charge of Your Time" seeks to explore the principles, practices, and benefits of time management in life and leadership. It seeks to express the findings of biblical study, proven principles, best practices, and decades of personal experience in the trenches. You may be at the front end of your journey seeking to be a disciplined student, or a senior minister seeking to affirm or add to your gathered wealth of knowledge. You may undertake valuable self-assessment of your priorities and activities or develop strategies toward truly "having the time of your life!" As related to servant leadership, it is not too much to claim that time management is self-leadership in the eternal service of Christ, who admonished, "Work for the night is coming when no man can work."

TIME TO FOCUS

"Time management is really a misnomer, because we all have exactly the same amount of time... Self-management is a better term...Most people manage their lives by crises...Effective time managers are opportunity-minded. The essence of time management is to set priorities and then to organize and execute around them."

From Stephen R. Covey,
Principle-Centered Leadership

1. What Does This Time Book Seek to Offer?

- **Understanding:** To add to your understanding of time management as a critical component of practicing servant leadership in your life and ministry.

- **Diagnosis:** To aid you in making an assessment of your present time management skills and actual practices, and to identify areas where you have room to improve.

- **Practical application**: Although exegesis instruction, explanation, and theory are relied on throughout these pages, more than 100 skills and practices are recorded for your review and application. If even five of them are actually helpful in your practices, the book is worth your time.

- **Reflection, even planning:** To broaden your choice of strategies to take charge of your schedule, your priorities, and your leadership. These chapters should help you develop at least specific actions that will make a difference in your life and your leadership. What if you could "rescue from drowning" only five hours each week? What could those 15 days for reallocation contribute toward your quality of life?

- **Resources:** To serve as a "toolbox" of reference materials, including planning worksheets, and other helpful "timely" resources you can use again and again in developing your own time management effectiveness strategies. Hopefully, there will be something here for you!

2. What Is "Taking Charge of Your Time," or Time Management?

- Taking charge of your time is living with a purpose. It is life management!

- It is living in trust. You are not required to do it all yourself. Your confidence in those around you will help you, and empower them.

- It is living with self-understanding. Know how you spend your time as you continually reevaluate; be aware of your own needs for balance in life.

- Taking charge of your time is about doing the right things, not doing the most things.

> **KEY TEXT—Psalm 31:14-15**
>
> *But I trust in you, O Lord; I say, "You are my God." My times are in your hands; deliver me from my enemies and from those who pursue me.*

- It is planning: both long-term and short-term. It is more than scheduling, but it does include that.

- It creates balance: life is about depth and perspective, not just sequence.

- Taking charge of your time requires action; your plan must be followed.

- It is placing your time, your life, in the hands of God.

- Add from your own understanding and practices.

3. Time Management as a Process and Journey

The thesis and process of "Taking Charge of Your Time," or "having the time of your life," provides for time improvement through several approaches, each approach intersecting with the others. Learn from one of the following topics, or each one of them as needed. Like your life, it is more like a journey than a short sprint. So, the components or skills are listed separately and in an order, but that's because they cannot be crammed into one long paragraph. Take a glance at this development:

- Taking Charge: "What does it mean to be responsible, to live my life on purpose?"

- Biblical concepts of time: "What does Holy Scripture teach me about "time"?

- Taking a time inventory: "How do I presently use my time in life and ministry?"

- Developing a time-use plan: the ground floor: "What three foundation principles should I rely on?"

- Developing a time-use plan: "How do I get specific until it helps, in the right way?"

- Scheduling your time: "When do I actually do my life and ministry stuff?"

TIME TO FOCUS

Stephen R. Covey in *Principle-Centered Leadership*, p. 47, underscores the need for improvement: *"Associated with Habit #7: Sharpen the Saw is the unique endowment of continuous improvement or self-renewal to overcome entropy."*

꙳ Overcoming time-wasters: "How do I take charge over my time opponents?"

꙳ Making time for your ministry: "Do I save, or make time for ministry functions?"

4. Personal Reflections and Warm-Up Questions

TIME TO FOCUS

Leo Tolstoy, famed Russian novelist, is quoted as saying, *"There is only one time that is important— NOW! It is the most important time because it is the only time that we have any power."*

What we do with the time we have is the agenda of time management. If we were in a conference together, we might begin by asking a few "warm-up" questions—for getting acquainted and identifying specific applications. Let's try it here, ok? Respond to the questions that apply to you:

꙳ Do you have good time-use practices that could be affirmed in this study?

꙳ What is your most immediate interest or need for time management? Is there a particular weak point in your leadership strategy? A particular circumstance that needs a remedy? A general feeling about your time use? Or maybe it's yet-to-be determined?

꙳ When you think about "time management," what comes to mind? Consider two or three key ideas that might guide your quest.

⤳ Who do you know that seems to be a good example of effective time management? What characteristics led you to that conclusion? Do you follow that example?

⤳ What questions do you have about your own leadership practices? Do you already have a sense of how managing your time differently could answer those questions?

⤳ Time-bind list: What are your 3 to 5 most pressing, challenging time management needs? Keep these in mind; talk them over with others.

⤳ Notes: Keep these warm-up thoughts in mind as you work through these chapters, but maintain openness for incorporating new concerns, new opportunities for improvement, and a fresh perspective on your life and leadership. Leadership training isn't just about considering new answers to the difficult questions you have been facing in your ministry; it's also the process of learning new questions!

5. Time Management Expresses Servant Leadership

In another SkillTrack publication focusing on "your journey toward servant leadership," the following definition and graphic is presented and encouraged.

TIME TO FOCUS

"Practicing servant leadership is self-giving service with others after the pattern of Jesus Christ in order to achieve through example and persuasion, extraordinary commitment and contributions toward mutually shared kingdom goals."

Lloyd Elder

Even in time management, we cannot allow ourselves to wander away from the main thing about ministry leadership—being a servant leader after the pattern of Jesus Christ. Taking Charge of your Time is one of the skills found to be most important to every leader in every field of endeavor. In fact, time management contributes to all five practices of servant leadership that we have explored: **empowered, ethical, enabling (or, equipping), effective leadership,** and **efficient leadership**. By contributing to "efficient leadership," your use of time, in reality, enriches all five components of servant leadership. Living your life on purpose is essential to daily performance.

Since time management is a leadership skill having to do with "life management," it is worthy of focused attention and investment. The servant leadership graphic provides a viewpoint important for every part of time management. Reflect often on the goal of following the pattern of Christ, who told His disciples to "work for the night is coming when no one can work."

6. Putting Yourself in the Timeframe—Reflection and Self-Assessment

Step into the picture with me and Mark Short who was my trusted friend and fellow minister for three decades. I learned much from him. During his lifetime of distinguished leadership and service, Mark was a constant student of Christian ministry and its demands. He published an excellent manual regarding time management, one of few written specifically for ministers to help with the practice of time management. His widow, Margie, was pleased to give permission to have these brief concepts reported and adapted in my teaching assignments and publications.

Upon reflection you may find that his insights (embedded with my own) identify with your own experiences and findings. You may also be encouraged to find that such concepts and habits are already being practiced in your life and work. A statement of Short's philosophy is a good starting point calling for each minister to develop a sound philosophy for the practice of time management. He has written:

TIME MANAGEMENT SURVEY from *Leadership Magazine*
www.ctlibrary.com/le/spring/812086.html

Are your management traits and needs similar to the 600 pastors responding to a recent national survey?

- Most pastors have little or no training in time management and are having to learn to "work smarter" by trial and error.

- More than one-third do not use any time-management tool.

- Despite perceptions to the contrary, there's not much difference in the way large-church pastors spend their time, compared to pastors who have no staff support.

- Regardless of the church or staff size, pastors reported spending about 11 hours each week in sermon preparation.

- Most satisfied pastors share common traits: limit their work to 45 to 50 weekly hours; have learned to live with unfinished business; use all their annual vacation; consistently take one full day off each week.

- Many pastors desire to learn more about managing time.

> *The minister who best utilizes the gift of time will develop a philosophy of time that assures the best use of each day. A conscious effort to constantly establish priorities in light of predetermined goals is essential. It is imperative that the minister understands that good time management aids success, while improper time management leads to failure.*

> *Everyone has twenty-fours in a day. Why then do some people seem to accomplish so much more? We rationalize that another minister can get by on only six hours of sleep a night. Or, he has a big staff. Excuse-making will not relieve us of our responsibility in wisely using time! We can do all the things we really need to do if we approach time management properly. Remember, you will manage your time, or it will manage you.*

Practical Concepts: Short's book is biblical, brief, practical, and thoroughly researched. It explores 10 topics on time management, each one of significant help to the minister. Content includes the following topics:

1. *The minister and time management*
2. *A time analysis*
3. *Successful scheduling*
4. *The organized minister*
5. *Coming to grips with procrastination*
6. *Learning to delegate*
7. *Decisions and time management*
8. *Effective meetings*
9. *Planning for leisure*
10. *The Christian concept of time*

And now in closing, consider using the following assessment form: 1) copy this page; 2) enlarge it to a full page size; 3) read over the list of 25 functions and practices; 4) rate your current skill level, 1=poor to 4=excellent; 5) score your performance as instructed on the form; 6) edit the form to include any additional ministry functions; 7) use the outcome of the assessment to enhance your personal learning curve.

TAKING CHARGE of Your *Time* & Stress

MINISTER'S TIME MANAGEMENT ASSESSMENT FORM
by Lloyd Elder, Th.D. adapted from *Time Management for Ministers*, pp. 21-22
by Mark Short, Nashville: Convention Press, 1987 (119 pages)

Using this form, take a snapshot of your practice of time management; it may affirm strengths or point out needed improvements. Be candid with yourself as you appraise your time habits, as if someone were looking over your shoulder. Print a copy and circle each item from 1 (poor) to 4 (excellent); then, score your responses at the close.

1.	I have clearly written objectives/goals.	1 2 3 4
2.	I set my priorities and stick to them.	1 2 3 4
3.	I do advance planning on my personal schedule.	1 2 3 4
4.	I consistently balance my work and personal schedules.	1 2 3 4
5.	I regularly write daily "to-do" lists.	1 2 3 4
6.	I avoid "blind alleys" and time-wasters.	1 2 3 4
7.	I have a keen sense of my life's purpose.	1 2 3 4
8.	I regularly delegate tasks to others.	1 2 3 4
9.	I practice an effective decision-making process.	1 2 3 4
10.	I can easily retrieve needed material.	1 2 3 4
11.	I set deadlines and meet them.	1 2 3 4
12.	I try to leave my work at work.	1 2 3 4
13.	I can usually facilitate casual "drop-in" people.	1 2 3 4
14.	I maintain a pocket calendar/"day timer"/ "I-Phone."	1 2 3 4
15.	I allow time for emergencies/opportunities.	1 2 3 4
16.	I know the "time zone" for my best work.	1 2 3 4
17.	I tackle my most important task in my "time zone."	1 2 3 4
18.	I usually do not delay problem solving.	1 2 3 4
19.	I batch or organize my tasks for better use of time.	1 2 3 4
20.	I am on time for 9 out of 10 of my engagements.	1 2 3 4
21.	I include professional development in my schedule.	1 2 3 4
22.	I have a regular physical exercise program.	1 2 3 4
23.	I have a regular meditation/devotional time.	1 2 3 4
24.	I make meetings meaningful and productive.	1 2 3 4
25.	My task assignments are mirrored in my work schedule.	1 2 3 4

Your Assessment Total _____

Assessment Scoring: Add your circled numbers together and select your time management assessment. This is your snapshot estimate; refer to it throughout the study.

✓　85–100: Excellent time manager; may be too time-conscious.
✓　65–84: Good time manager; pick your practices to improve.
✓　45–64: Improvement needed; give time-use a higher priority.
✓　25–44: Get help; there's a better world out there for you.

CHAPTER 2
Living with Four Biblical Concepts of Time, for Today

When we think of "time" in the Bible, it usually brings to mind ancient history, early civilizations and antiquity, writings and events from "a long time ago." It is easy to let such a concept of "time" become the great distance between ourselves and the teachings of Holy Scripture! But Scripture offers a rich array of ways to understand and utilize "time," all of which can contribute to your study of time management. Toward the front of our exploration, looking first at biblical concepts of time will give you a strong foundation for time management. You may find that "time" closes, not widens, the gap between Holy text and your life today. As we look back to the bible, let us keep in mind the variety of ways we use the concepts and words of "Time."

GLOSSARY: "TIME" (contemporary uses)
from *The American Heritage® Dictionary*

A non-spatial continuum from the past through the present to the future.

➤ *An interval separating two points on this continuum; a duration.*

➤ *A number, as of years, days, or minutes, of such an interval.*

➤ *An interval, especially a span of years, marked by similar events, conditions; an era.*

➤ *Times—the present with respect to prevailing conditions and trends: a suitable or opportune moment or season.*

➤ *An appointed or fated moment, especially of death or giving birth.*

➤ *One's lifetime, one's period of greatest activity or engagement.*

Four Biblical Meanings of Time: This chapter encourages you to "have the time of your life" in the deepest possible sense. It means more than just planning your day and week efficiently (though that certainly is a big part of it for most of us). Consider carefully the depth of biblical "time" as outlined here. It is a first big step toward understanding the power and significance of your time. You may want to log your own thoughts and experiences!

As we investigate four significant ways Scripture presents "time" and its primary words, follow the storyline and its Scripture, commentary and glossary references as you consider your own meanings, even experiences of "time." Have you been thinking broadly enough to respond to the challenges of Scripture? Which areas of "time" have you been neglecting? Record your thoughts as you review.

A Clock as a Time Visual—Limited but Helpful? The following graphic has a limited purpose. What does it intend to portray, and what doesn't it? It intends to convey that in the biblical texts, Old and New Testaments alike, **time hangs together in one whole—it is holistic.** The "time piece" of history cannot be broken apart. The four primary meanings of time, the few words most directly used, and the large number of related terms—all merge and converge to tell one biblical story from beginning to end. But there are levels of perspective, experience, and even significance. There are historical sequences, moments of extraordinary opportunity, markers of fulfillment, and a great and eternal that is here and now and yet out yonder. The clock as a time piece stands only as a symbol of the whole, but so could a sun dial, an hour glass, or a calendar. Let's take up the pieces to help us grasp, and act upon the whole.

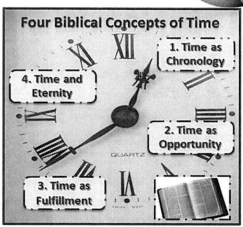

Four Biblical Concepts of Time

1. Time as Chronology
4. Time and Eternity
2. Time as Opportunity
3. Time as Fulfillment

1. Time as Chronology—*"chronos"*

"Time is God's way of keeping everything from happening at once." This quip from an unknown source sums up the impact of the biblical concept of time as chronology; time sets out the sequence and duration of moments and the centuries. The Bible speaks of time as "chronology" when measuring the linear passing of time—as references to the sequence and duration of events. A person's life-span, a season, a progression of occurrences, all fall under this category. This terminology also uses *"chronos"* to mark certain time periods by associating them with individuals or events ("the time of Abraham," etc.).

> **John 14:9** (NIV) *Jesus answered: "Don't you know me, Philip, even after I have been among you such a long time? Anyone who has seen me has seen the Father. How can you say, 'Show us the Father'?"*

> **Acts 1:7** (NIV) *He said to them: "It is not for you to know the times or dates the Father has set by his own authority."*

> **Glossary**: "chronology" (from <u>WordNet</u>® 1.6, ©1997 Princeton University) *1: arrangement of events in time 2: a record of events in the order of their occurrence 3: the determination of the actual temporal sequence of past events.*

Reflection: *When you plan your annual calendar or your to-do list for a day, you are doing "Chronos" work. However, you are also making judgments about the use of your time and making contributions toward the balance, priority, and purpose of your life. When you contemplate about "the seasons of a man's life," or simply reflect on generation gaps or the aging process, you are also working with chronology time.*

2. Time as Opportunity—"*kairos*"

Scripture refers to time as opportunity when speaking not of a particular moment in time, but of the proper moment, the appointed time, "just the right time." God as the creator of all time has directed the celestial bodies, the seasons, the festivals and days of rest for mankind. These appointed proper moments in the personal events of your life and epoch periods of history, give us the opportunity to interact with God's creation in making the best possible use of time. "*Kairos*" is time that calls for decisions, that demands action—either through **crisis or opportunity**—and thus refers to the "what should be done now" more than just to the "when to do this, now or later." See Ephesians 5:15-16, Acts 3:19.

> ↝ **Ephesians 5:15-16** (NIV) *"Be very careful, then, how you live—not as unwise but as wise, making the most of every opportunity [time], because the days are evil."*

> ↝ **Zondervan Commentary** on Eph. 5:15-16: *What is meant is simply to make the best possible use of all circumstances like prudent merchants. Kairos ("opportunity," NIV) is the right moment, which Paul urges his readers to grasp lest it be wasted.*

> ↝ **Glossary**: opportunity (from <u>Webster's Revised Unabridged Dictionary</u>) *1. Fit or convenient time; a time or place favorable for executing a purpose; a suitable combination of conditions; suitable occasion; chance.*

Reflection: When you break into your planned sermon study time to answer miscellaneous telephone calls, you are disrupting an intentional decision to be prepared when it is time to preach. But, when you drop everything and rush to the emergency room because a church family has been in a major auto accident, you are making a "kairos" decision. As well, when you decline a desirable dinner date because your daughter is starring in her 6th grade school play, you are seizing an opportune time in your family.

When you set out to challenge your congregation to make changes and take responsibility for their present opportunities, you might be expressing this concept of time. Let me fashion such a biblical concept from my years of pastoring.

> *"This is God's time for us in his service. Others have gone before us and served mightily. They have assessed their times and found ways to be faithful to Christ's cause. Some of them are now in the heavenly stadium*

*of the faithful. We too have seen God do great things with us and through us. Now, **this is our time. It is our watch on the wall of the house of God.** It will take hard work and obedient faith. How then shall we live and how shall we respond to the call of the Lord? We must rise to the magnitude of opportunity. We too must assess our time and the calling of God, claim his promises and resources and move forward into his bright day before us. Will we do it? With all my heart I believe we will—together."*

3. Time as Fulfillment

The Bible speaks of time as the fulfillment promises or prophecies of an age which will, or has already, come to pass. The Old Testament prophets speak not only of a particular "time" but of the time of the coming of God's Kingdom, an assured promise of judgment and salvation. In the New Testament, that time has arrived with the coming of Christ. This "time" is a realization and fulfillment by which all other time is to be measured. Examples:

- ⤳ **Mark 1:15** (NIV) *"The time has come" he said. "The kingdom of God is near. Repent and believe the good news."* <u>Commentary</u>: *Mark 1:15 (from Zondervan Commentary) Time here is not simply chronological time (chronos) but the decisive time (kairos) for God's action... He marks the fulfillment of the special salvation-time which is distinguished from all other time.*

- ⤳ **Galatians 4:4-5** (NIV) *But when the time had fully come, God sent his Son, born of a woman, born under law, to redeem those under law, that we might receive the full rights of sons.* <u>Commentary</u>: *Gal. 4:4-5 (from Zondervan Commentary) It was a time when the pax Romana extended over most of the civilized earth; when travel and commerce were therefore possible; ... great roads linked the empire of the Caesars, ... far more significantly by the all-pervasive language of the Greeks. Add the fact that the world was sunk in a moral abyss so low that even the pagans cried out against it and that spiritual hunger was everywhere evident.... Viewed theologically, however, it may also be said that the time was full because God himself had filled it with meaning.*

Reflection: When you stake your life and your ministry on the fulfillment of the coming of Christ the Redeemer, you are expressing your confidence in God's timing and your place in it. When you preach from the Old Testament about the fulfillment of prophecy of the coming of the Christ, and you are rely on the New Testament as a primary source for interpretation, you are acknowledging the time concept of "fulfillment."

4. Time and Eternity

Eternity is a complicated conception! Bible versions often translate a language phrase "into the ages of the ages" with one word, either as "eternal," or "everlasting." Often Scriptures set eternity and time apart as opposite: "eternity," the state of God's being, and "time," the state of man's existence. Eternity is also linked to time, for example, when referring to the end of man's time, the coming of eternity. Better yet, eternity can be understood as a quality of time: we will both experience eternal life in our own historic timeframe by accepting Christ and following His path, and also throughout the eternal ages with Christ. See Revelation 10:6 and 2 Corinthians 4:28.

> **Commentary**: 2 Cor. 4:18 (from Zondervan Commentary) *Behind the contrast ... is the Pauline tension between the "already" and the "not yet," the contrast between what is now seen by mortals and what is as yet hidden from mortal gaze.... Paul was profoundly aware that the present age is transient (cf. 2 Cor. 7:31), whereas the age to come is eternal in the sense of being "destined to last forever," and that his afflictions were temporary but his reward eternal.*

> **Revelation 10:6** (NIV) *And he swore by him who lives for ever and ever, who created the heavens and all that is in them, the earth and all that is in it, and the sea and all that is in it, and said, "There will be no more delay [time]!"*

> **Glossary**: "eternity" (from Webster's Revised Unabridged Dictionary) *1. Infinite duration, without beginning in the past or end in the future; also, duration without end in the future; endless time. 2. Condition which begins at death; immortality.*

Reflection: Who can doubt that believers in every age have lived out the years of their lives with an ennobling view of the eternal, sometimes symbolized by the reality of heaven? In New Testament texts the eternal is blended with the continuing vision of the living Christ in our midst. When you live with confidence in the eternal saving and keeping power of God, you labor with more purpose until he comes. When you work faithfully in Christ's kingdom, you are living inside the eternal, more than spending time speculating about the time of His coming. A 19th century Irish lyric, translated by Mary E. Byrne, became a beloved early 20th century hymn of hope and adoration:

> *"Be Thou my vision, O Lord of my heart; naught be all else to me, save that Thou art; Thou my best thought, by day or by night; waking or sleeping Thy presence my light."*

Our lives may not be as dramatic as those of Paul or John, but they are of the same fabric of God's kind of time. We too are sometimes transformed by the living presence of the eternal:

- **Paul the Apostle from a prison cell:** *"I have fought the good fight, I have finished the race, I have kept the faith. Now there is in store for me the crown of righteousness, which the Lord, the righteous Judge, will award me on that day—and not only to me, but also to all who have longed for his appearing."* **(2 Tim. 4:7-8 NIV)**

- **John of the Revelation, exiled on the island of Patmos:** *"On the Lord's Day I was in the spirit, and I heard behind me a loud voice like a trumpet… (Rev. 1:10) "He who testifies to these things says, 'yes, I am coming soon.' Amen. Come, Lord Jesus."* **(Rev. 22:20)**

Closing Reflections

- Review major texts on "time" using your own Bible and Bible dictionary.

- Develop your own "Biblical Basis for Time Management." Keep it short and personal.

- In your time management, give attention to the four views of time. What would you continue the same? What should you change?

- The following Study Abstract is provided to refer you to one of many good resources.

A Study Abstract prepared by Lloyd Elder:

"TIME" BY E. JENNI
Interpreter's Dictionary of the Bible, Vol. R-Z
Nashville: Abingdon Press, 1962 (from pp. 643-649)

To understand the biblical concept of time, one must take care not to assume unconsciously our modern Western scientific or philosophical interpretation of time in the Bible or to carry it over into the Bible. The Bible itself becomes the benchmark of its meaning of "time":

1. **Terminology**—Only the more important and more general concepts of time are discussed in this article.

   - In biblical Hebrew. The Hebrew Old Testament has no general word for "time," and likewise no special term for the categories of time—past, present, future. The most widely used word translated as "time" is *eth* (about 290 times); it means—not time in its duration—but rather, the moment or point of time that something happens (Ex. 9:18). It may also indicate the suitable, favorable time (II Sam. 11:1); or in eschatological context the coming hour of judgment (Is. 13:22). The OT has not developed a special term for "eternity" which one could contrast with "temporality."

   - In Septuagint Greek. There is a general word for "space of time"—"time": *chronos*; used as a measurable quantity. It also uses *kairos* to mean point of time (Heb. *eth*). The word *aion* originally means "vital force," "life," then "age," "lifetime."

   - In New Testament Greek., *Chronos* is comparatively rare—measurable duration (Mt. 25:19). In using *hamera*, "day" for point of time (Mt. 26:29), the NT follows the Hebrew-Aramaic usage. The word *kairos* signals opportunity or God-given possibility (Heb. 11:15). The use of the word *aion* as in LXX means "long, distant, uninterrupted time" (Luke 1:70).

2. **In the Old Testament**

   - The events and their time constitute, to a large extent, a time unit in the OT (Gen. 1:5). On the whole, then, one must probably assume that the OT had an unconsidered chronological, linear conception of time.

   - Time and revelation. The OT attests God's action of revelation in history and thus in time (Isa. 24-27); this interpretation as the history of salvation had an influence on the understanding of time.

   - God and time (eternity). God's dominion over time is most clearly revealed by the fact that He created time along with the universe as its creature form of existence (Gen. 1).

   - Man and time. Temporality is the God-given form of existence for the creature world (Job 1:21); man is not immortal (Gen. 3:22).

3. **In the New Testament**

   - The NT builds on the OT understanding of time, which is linear, and bears the stamp of the story of salvation; and develops it further, consistently. All expressions of Christian faith are temporal, are decidedly in time.

↪ The salvation-historical view is basic everywhere: expressed in the redemptive significance of the incarnation of Christ; of His unique dying and subsequent resurrection; and of His *parousia*—the day of Christ in the future.

↪ Mark 1:15—*"The time is fulfilled, and the kingdom of God is at hand; repent, and believe the gospel."* The present *kairos*, "constantly pending decision," includes expectation of a future realization. The mission of Christ was in the fullness of time (Eph. 1:10), and His work was

CHAPTER 3
Taking Your Own Time Inventory
A First Action Step

KEY TEXT—Psalm 90:10, 12

The length of our days is seventy years—or eighty, if we have the strength; yet their span is but trouble and sorrow, for they quickly pass, and we fly away... Teach us to number our days aright, that we may gain a heart of wisdom.

Personal Introduction

"**H**ow many of you have ever helped to take an inventory?"** Wow! Did that question ever get a wild discussion started? Through the years, when I come to this time inventory stuff, I usually start with that question. One such time was in Dallas, my home town by the way, at a minister training conference and many jumped in with their experiences. **Stream of Responses:** *"Yea I have, and it was boring." "Me too, I hired on to be a salesman, not as a parts counter and shelf duster." "I'm glad we did it only once a year." "I liked to do inventory because we were paid overtime." "It was interesting, I kinda' got a larger picture of the company's business." "I was an inventory manager, so it was absolutely essential to my job."*

Why does a business do a regular inventory? The ministers seemed to respond in support of the thesis: "Regular inventory is essential to first-rate company operation." Such responses were expressed as **questions,** such as: Just how large is company inventory? Does it meet the inventory business plan? Is the company over-invested in inventory? Are we out of any particular product, or even very low? Do we have an unacceptable backorder? Are we carrying obsolete stock? Is the inventory in good shape, ready to ship out? Has there been unaccountable shrinkage? Why and how? Is there a new opportunity, a possible gap in the product line? Do we need to rearrange the storeroom space, or even have a clearance sale? What products are actually selling, contributing to company profit?

GLOSSARY: "INVENTORY"
from *The American Heritage® Dictionary*

1) A detailed, itemized list, report, or record of things in one's possession, especially a periodic survey of goods and materials in stock; the process of making such a list of the quantity of goods and materials on hand. 2) An evaluation or a survey, as of abilities, assets, or resources.

Now, back to the primary focus: ministers taking a time management inventory? An essential step toward developing personal time management strategies is to take a self-inventory of your time. Becoming honestly aware of your present practice will

---

TIME TO FOCUS

Peter Drucker on Time Inventory: *"Effective execu-tives, in my observation, do not start with their tasks. They start with their time.... They start by finding out where their time actually goes. This three-step process includes: recording time; managing time; and consolidating time."* (Drucker, p. 25)

illuminate your constraints, your shortcomings, and your opportunities for synchronizing your life mission with your daily activities. In <u>The Effective Executive</u> (a leadership book I started using four decades ago) Peter Drucker has an excellent chapter titled, "Know Thy Time."

This chapter emphasizes a time inventory on three levels to be investigated in the following material:

- **Measurement**—"How much time is there?" Each day, everyone seemingly has the same amount of time; it is truly a limited resource.

- **Accounting**—"How do you actually spend your time?" Logging how you actually spend your time is the most important self-revelation you can make in your time inventory.

- **Pricing**—"How much is your time worth?" Whether you realize it or not, your time does come at a cost. Is a particular activity worth the cost of doing it? Could it be delegated to someone else? Would a cost-efficient method help? Should it simply be left undone?

1. Measuring Your Time—"How much time do you have?"

How many years in a life? How many hours in a week? Our task as servant leaders for Christ is to be good stewards of whatever time we do have. You may often opine, "I just wish I had more time!" But it doesn't really help. You and I cannot invent more time or save it up. Time is quite a limited, finite resource, at least in this transitory segment of our lives! How much time do you have? Seemingly we never have enough, but scan these obvious units of time:

> *One life to live*
> *One year at a time*
> *Four seasons to enjoy*
> *Twelve months to plan*
> *Fifty two weeks and 365 days*
> *8,760 hours, 525,600 minutes and 31, 536,000 seconds*

Whether or not you have ever helped to take any other kind of inventory, the purpose and benefits of "taking inventory" illustrate the front end of time management: "How much time do you have" —only one life, one moment at a time? From an old adage about the use of money, let me paraphrase an old rhyme with new words about time:

> **"It's not what you'd do with decades**
>
> **If old-age were to be your lot.**
>
> **It's what you're doing this moment**
>
> **With the only time you've got."**

This "time ditty" may oversimplify the concept of measuring your time, but it does focus on the need to be specific about time issues. What are you doing with your time—starting now?

2. Accounting for Time—"How do you spend your total time?"

Begin to think about how you use your day. Using these broad categories of functions, estimate how you allocate the 24 hours in an average day. Save the detailed accounting for later—we'll get to that next! When you're satisfied with your estimation in all of the categories, add them up—and then level them out to be a whopping 168 hours a week. You'll want to return to this when you're building your time-use plan.

One national survey indicates that the average work-week for professionals and executives is 54-56 hours. More recently, a survey discovered a 41-hour work week. How does this compare to your practice? Thomas A. Edison died in 1931 at age 84. He had said, *"I'm long on ideas, but short on time. I expect to live to be only about a hundred."*

The next pages ask you to estimate how you use your total time of 168 hours per week. You could just guess at your time-use for a "normal" week (if such exists). Most of us do. To evaluate and clarify your numbers, create a time-use log sheet by dividing your days into 30 minute blocks. Assign each block to one of the categories below based on how you spend your time; do it every day for a week. Copy, edit if necessary, and write in your estimated response for the weekly totals in the form below.

WEEKLY TIME INVENTORY FORM
168 Hours
(Copy this form, edit as needed and est. hours)

CATEGORY	EST. HOURS
Personal: *all things for personal upkeep*	
Sleep/Rest: *intentional at regular times*	
Family: *being together, planned or spontaneous*	
Spiritual: *quiet time, reading, prayer, reflection*	
Secular Work: *full or part-time, incl. driving time*	
Church Ministry: *total on the job, continuous, or split shift*	
Other:	
Other:	
Other:	
Other:	
Other:	
Other:	
Other:	

Weekly Total Hours   168

TAKING CHARGE of Your *Time & Stress*

MINISTRY TIME INVENTORY FORM
Est. Weekly Hours
(Copy, edit as needed, and est. hours; save this for Ministry Planning)

TASKS/FUNCTIONS	EST. HOURS
Worship/Preaching:	
Education/Teaching:	
Evangelism/Witnessing:	
Pastoral Care/Visiting:	
Fellowship Building:	
Administration:	
Community/Missions:	
Denominational Service:	
Prof. Development:	
Other:	
Other:	
Other:	
Other:	
Est. Weekly Work Hours	

3. Accounting for Work Time—"How do you use your ministry time?"

Now, let's get more specific about an inventory of your ministry time—that is, from your log or making an estimate of how you are now using your weekly ministry time. Taking the daily estimate of ministry time from the previous form, determine how many weekly hours you spend in each of your paid ministry/leadership functions. Remember, surveys have come up with differing numbers on the minister's work-week, from 41 to 54 hours. If you can do a thoughtful estimate of the use of your time, you are well along on a first step to healthy time management. The Form below will give some ideas for developing work categories and estimates. Put everything else in the <u>other category</u>—but identify what all the "other" stands for!

4. Pricing Your Time—"What is your work-time worth?"

If you were asked, "Are you worth what you are being paid?" With or without being offended, you would be quick to answer, "Of course I am." Most of us give careful thought to spend our at-work time in functions and activities that are worth the compensation. We also give priority time to the priority functions required of our ministry position. Benjamin Franklin and others since then have proclaimed and we would agree, "Time is money."

But unlike money, it is not possible to save time—only to allocate it wisely. There is a way to calculate or at least estimate the compensation for the work hours of our ministry time. Let's give it a try. Copy, then enlarge and edit the form to fit your position description. It helps if you also gather two resources: a job description (or known expectations) of your ministry position, including the number of hours in your weekly schedule; and also a copy of your gross compensation. Fill in the following worksheet to calculate the cost of your work hours. If not, from your experience develop a list of your ministry employer's expectations. Change the categories listed below to reflect your assigned tasks and write in the numbers. Once you've completed this activity, the net cost/price of each hour of your ministry/work will be estimated at the bottom of the table. Do you spend wisely each hour?

CALCULATION OF COMPENSATION
PER WORK HOUR
(Copy, edit as needed)

ITEM	AMOUNT
1. Total Yearly Compensation $	$_____
Gross annual salary as a minister	$_____
Value of housing (or allowance)	$_____
Insurance, annuity, etc.	$_____
Other compensation	$_____
2. Estimate your annual ministry work hours	_____
Enter avg. work hours per week	_____
Multiplied by 52 weeks = hours per year	_____
(Divide annual compensation by annual work hours)	
Equals avg. cost of each work hour	$_____
(Also, you may calculate cost per week or month)	

Reflection/Application

This Time Inventory may be "for your eyes only;" or, you may decide that it fits your purpose to discuss it with a friend or mentor. However you chose to express your reflection, the following questions are primarily for your benefit:

- Does your time inventory indicate that you are living true to a worthy purpose?

- Does the way you spend your time represent a balanced life including family, personal, and your chosen ministry?

- Are you using your time to achieve desired results identified in your priorities?

- Are you using your work time in a way that represents your assignments and tasks?

- Do you spend most of your "at-work" hours in ways that return a "fair market value" to your church or other employer?

CHAPTER 4
Developing Time-Use Planning
Foundation Principles and
Specific Practices

S tarting "from the ground up," suggests that you start your time-use planning with strong foundations: such as purpose, balance and priorities. One of the easiest ways to get into deep water with your time management, and life management, is by scheduling and planning first from the smallest, most pressing things. Everything seems to clamor, "do me first." Do you find yourself making "to-do" lists to cover all the little things for the day, while the big things get put on hold? We all do that in one way or another.

Why not bring your time-use planning into harmony with your life principles by planning from the ground up, starting with the big things first! The premise of this chapter, drawn from leading time management experts today, is that "having the time of your life" requires you to start with fundamental decisions about your life and work, and build upon that foundation:

- **Purpose:** What is your life mission? Ultimately, your sense of mission in life should guide how you spend your time.

- **Balance:** Is your total life in balance? The result of good time management should be a balanced, quality personal, family, and work life.

⤳ **Priorities:** What key life/ministry activities will help you achieve your purpose and keep your life in balance?

⤳ **Practices:** Three supporting practices that help to implement each principle.

Time-Use Principles

© LEA, Inc.

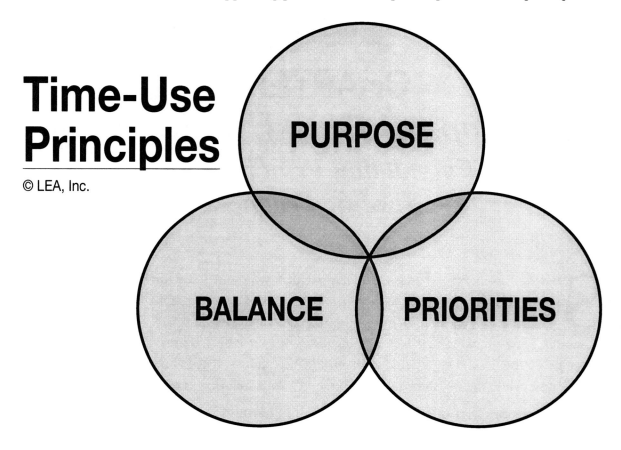

PURPOSE

BALANCE

PRIORITIES

Principle #1—Purpose: What is your life mission?

What kind of life do you want to lead? What principles are at the heart of your ministry and leadership roles? What ideas, institutions, and relationships have your truest commitment? Your time use should be congruent with your highest intentions about life. In First Things First, Stephen R. Covey lists elements of an *"empowering mission statement."*

On these pages, or in a personal journal, review or construct a personal mission statement. Read Covey's list for basic guidance. Try to devise a succinct and honest account

EMPOWERING MISSION STATEMENT
by Stephen Covey

- *Represents the deepest and best within you.*

- *Is the fulfillment of your own unique gifts.*

- *Is transcendent; it's based on principles of contribution and purpose higher than self.*

- *Includes fulfillment in physical, social, mental, and spiritual dimension.*

- *Is based on principles that produce quality-of-life results.*

- *Deals with both vision and principle-based values; an empowering mission statement deals with both character and competence.*

- *Deals with all the significant roles in your life; it represents a lifetime balance of personal, family, work, community.*

- *Is written to inspire you—not to impress anyone else.*

[from *First Things First* by Stephen Covey, p. 113]

---

of the life you want to live. Try not to worry about scheduling, even priorities just yet. Think big principles—in your life, your leadership, and your ministry.

Reflection: When I served as a pastor in the 1950's, we had a Vacation Bible School motto (adapted from John Wesley) that I accepted as my life purpose. It has served me well throughout the years: *"I will do the best I can, with what I have, where I am, for as long as I can, for Jesus' sake today!"* As you work on your own life mission statement, consider what John Wesley, renowned in history for his methodical practice of biblical pietism, admonishes:

> John Wesley: *"Do all the good you can, in all the ways you can, to all the souls you can, in every place you can, at all the times you can, with all the zeal you can, as long as ever you can."*

Principle #2—Balance: Is your total life in balance?

If you just completed a life mission statement and feel a sense of neglect over one or more areas of your life that you identified as essential, you are not alone. As you begin to put your life and work into a sharper focus, the contrast between priority and reality can be startling, even painful. Jesus, in His great love commandment, fixed in place a type of balanced life plan: *"Love the Lord your God with all your heart, soul, mind, and strength"* and the second is like that, love your neighbor as yourself (from Luke 10:27; also see Luke 2:52). Let's turn the findings of the time-use inventory and the call for a balanced, wholeness of life into reality with the actions we take!

Your Time Balancing Act

- ✤ *Sleep / Rest*
- ✤ *Spiritual Growth*
- ✤ *Personal Time*
- ✤ *Family Time*
- ✤ *Secular Work*
- ✤ *Retirement*
- ✤ *Christian Ministry*
- ✤ *Community Service*

Where does your life need more balance? The elements of your life may differ from another person's; but, the need for balance applies to all! It may be just as important for your well-being as the activities that fill your time. The choices you make—based on your purpose, values, priorities, and expectations—all contribute to that balancing act that is your life and leadership in ministry.

Reflection on Your Balancing Act

- Does your own self-assessment show the need for greater balance? Record your thoughts here or in your personal journal along with your personal mission statement. We're still not at the scheduling stage.

- Make commitments to yourself about your life balance. Begin sentences with "I should spend more time doing…" and "I could spend less time…"

- Striking a balance between work and personal life is a process that requires a partnership between the manager and the employee (ministry leader and team).

- As you think about your own life and ministry, how can you put these first two principles into practice?

  - Read, review, and apply these fundamental principles immediately, and start with yourself—now.

  - Adopt or adapt them as practices in your own total life traffic pattern.

  - Share the practices with at least one key person, to broaden that person's time-use balance.

  - Make these principles part of your church/staff philosophy and expectations of employees.

  - In addition to your leadership role, apply the principles to your other roles: personal, family, school, neighbor, professional groups, etc.

  - This does not diminish your Christian work ethic, but it does put work into the perspective of your whole life.

TAKING CHARGE of Your *Time & Stress*

A Study Abstract prepared by Lloyd Elder:

A HARVARD BUSINESS REVIEW: On Work and Life Balance
Harvard Business School Press, 2000;
Article: "Work and Life" by Stewart D. Friedman, et. al., pp. 1-2, 27-29

This is a very substantive book with insightful review articles on the subject of time use; only the first article is introduced here, reflecting on both purpose and balance:

- Most companies view work and personal life as competing priorities in a zero-sum game, in which a gain in one area means a loss in the other.

- A new breed of managers, however, is trying a new tack, one in which managers and employees collaborate to achieve work and personal objectives to everyone's benefit.

- These managers are guided by three principles with an emphasis on "what is important:"

  - Clearly inform employees about business priorities and encourage them to be clear about personal priorities.

  - Recognize and support employees as whole persons, celebrating their roles outside of work.

  - Experiment with creative ways to get work done and to allow employees to pursue personal goals.

Principle #3—Establishing Priorities: What matters most in your life and work?

What activities matter most in your life/ministry? What key life/ministry priorities will help you achieve your purpose and keep your life in balance? With your mission statement and life-balance commitment in mind, what three to five priorities do you see before you during the next 12 months? Decide which functions and activities will most help you achieve that vision, either through a new commitment or a recommitment. Once you're satisfied with your thoughts on your priorities, write them down for your continued action planning.

TIME TO FOCUS

Golda Meir (1887-1978) reportedly expressed her practical perception of life priorities in a graphic way: *"I must govern the clock, not be governed by it."*

A Study Abstract prepared by Lloyd Elder:

HOW TO BALANCE COMPETING TIME DEMANDS
by Doug Sherman and William Hendricks
Colorado Springs: NavPress, 1989

"Keeping the Five Most Important Areas of Your Life in Perspective" requires balancing a "pentathlon" of personal life, family, work, church, and community. This is an annotated outline of a book on time management written from a Christian perspective. The purpose is twofold: (1) to introduce what the book presents; (2) to suggest issues you may face in building your own time management plan. The authors claim: This Is a Book for Busy People! If you're too busy to read this book, you need this book!

Part One: Is Your Life Out of Balance?

- We're All in This Together. No one escapes time demands. Here are some examples.

- Are You Stressed for Success? Our culture leaves God out of work—and gets work out of perspective as a result.

- What They don't Teach You in Sunday School. Christians have been taught an inadequate view of work—and that won't help them keep life in balance.

- You Can't Get There from Here! Three personal obstacles can deter you from enjoying life as it was meant to be lived.

Part Two: What Does It Mean to Balance Competing Time Demands?

- The Pentathlon: A New Way of Looking at Life. The Bible teaches a comprehensive view of life that helps us keep things in perspective.

- But Is the Pentathlon Valid? Don't take my word for it. The Pentathlon is right out of the Bible!

Part Three: Putting Work in Its Proper Perspective!

- "**APPLY**ing" the Pentathlon:

  - ❖ **A**—Analyze the Scriptures
  - ❖ **P**—Take a Personal Inventory
  - ❖ **P**—Plan Steps
  - ❖ **L**— Make Yourself Liable to Others
  - ❖ **Y**—Use Yardsticks to Measure Your Progress

- Watch Out for the Enemy!

- This All Sounds Good, But …

- Don't Stop Here! Apply the Pentathlon: A Manual for Growth

Do your larger priorities guide your daily choices of what is important, what needs to be done as the higher good? Stephen Covey reminds us that activities contributing to balance in life and in tune with our mission are a most important "true north" in a profound way. Why don't we do them all the time and nothing else? That's an excellent question for most of us. There are three potential counter-influences to doing the most important, most life-balancing things most of the time:

- operational assignments
- time-wasters
- urgent demands

Moving toward the important: What's true of most leaders is perhaps especially true of ministers: we don't feel in control of many of the pressing demands on our attention. Responding to urgency drives much of our day-to-day work. It is an essential function of leadership, not to be avoided; they don't call it "urgent" for nothing! But there may be ways to diminish the toll of stress and time that can occur when the urgent rules; for example:

- Learn to delegate! Do you try to take over every brush fire? Train and trust your team member to deal with many situations. This will help you build a competent, empowered team that will assume ownership of the ministry with the right encouragement!

- Develop efficient systems! Ever notice the urgent demands that keep coming up? Have procedures in place for dealing with crises. It will still require your attention, but the less you have to scramble for resources, the better.

- Practice good time habits: schedule time for the unknown in your planning. Keep organized notes in your file; don't make yourself relearn a situation every time it arises.

Ministry Time Management Matrix: The diagram below, an adaptation of Stephen Covey's "Time Management Matrix," divides activities into four quadrants—pairing the "urgent" and the "not urgent" with the "important" (in the deepest sense) and "not important." You spend some time in each section, but in which do you spend most of your time? Should you move more of your time toward the important? Are your principles reflected in your time decisions?

Ministry Time Management

	Urgent	Not Urgent
Important	**3. Crisis Ministry** • Crises, deaths, funerals • Deadlines • Pressing problems • Many meetings, appointments • Hospital calls, counseling • Other: ▶**High Stress/Burnout**	**4. Priority Ministry** • Strategic thinking, planning • Problem prevention • Seizing opportunities • Sermon / teaching preparation • Relationship building • Evangelistic efforts ▶**Productive/Satisfaction**
Not Important	**2. Controlled Ministry** • Membership demands • Interruptions • Some mail, reports, phone calls • Scheduled meetings • Many popular activities • Brush fires ▶ **Trapped/Driven**	**1. Trivial Pursuits** • Routine, busy work • Random mail, calls •Time-wasters • Many pleasant invitations • Procrastination activities • People distractions • Other: ▶ **Boredom/Wasted**

Ministry Time-Use Planning: How many hours do you plan to allocate per week toward each ministry function in order to live a productive, balanced life, following your priorities? **If you do not set your priorities and plan your schedule, others will do it for you.**

Principle #4—Developing Three Time-Use Practices

Practice follows principle. Principle #4 clusters three such practices in a supporting role: performance zones, task consolidation, and pacing yourself. With your personal foundation taking shape, turn your attention now to specific practices supporting those principles. These might be experienced as habits in your daily life, as well as contribute to your long- and short-term plans. Sometimes making your actions and your principles align in time management can be the most productive step of all.

Three Time-Use Practices: So, keep close your three critical principles—mission, balance, and priorities—while you explore these three exceptional practices:

Time-Use Practices

© LEA, Inc.

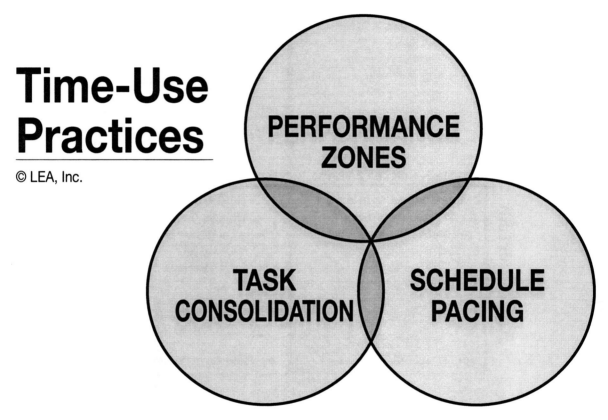

- **Performance zone:** discover when you are the most productive; an early morning riser, or late night closer? Then schedule your most demanding or creative work in this zone; don't attack random chores during those two to four hours.

- **Task consolidation:** run errands and meet appointments on a timed route; return six phone calls in one short chunk of time.

- **Pacing yourself:** Work at a project with concentration (say two hours), and then break your schedule into a less demanding task. Break your work down into blocks before a deadline.

Reflections: The following abstracts may enlarge your study or offer concepts and frameworks for your personal reflection and application.

A Study Abstract prepared by Lloyd Elder:

THE EXECUTIVE AT WORK: A Guide to Successful Performance
by Fred DeArmond: Englewood Cliffs, NJ:
Prentice-Hall, Inc., 1958, (from Chap. 7)

The Great American Alibi: "I'm too busy!" or "I haven't the time." It is offered as the excuse for all sorts of shortcomings. The president of a large company said that each day at least 3 executive hours out of 8 were nonproductive. Why? Examples:

- Waiting for a conference because someone is late: 12 minutes for 6 persons.
- A proud parent shows and introduces his boy around the office for 40 minutes.
- Looking for a lost chart removed from the file: 15 minutes for executive and secretary.
- Ten-minute coffee break stretched to 25 minutes to hear about the fishing trip.
- Two-hour luncheon to go across town and look at a hunting dog.
- One hour for writing a formal report when a 3-sentence memo would do.

Eliminate the Unessential—Arnold Bennett writes in <u>How to Live on 24 Hours a Day</u>:

- Don't be ruined by attempting too much and failing in the principle endeavor.
- Don't have too many outside interests, failing to stick to the main business.
- Take stock of waste motions—analyze how you use your time.
- Don't steal your time by over-listing, ready-volunteering, and extracurricular activities.
- Make more time for the essential things.
- Don't do things others can do for you.

Accent the Essential by Choosing, Planning, Concentrating

- Center on the present pain, not the headache to come or the next task.
- Be deliberate: don't tarry, don't hurry—avoid unnecessary mistakes.
- Escape the tyranny of the clock—don't be a clock watcher.
- When there's a big job to do, then do what must be done.
- Fill in those time interludes with short tasks that need to be done.
- Use your calendar pad—write it down, schedule, then make time to do it.

MORE →

TAKING CHARGE of Your *Time* & Stress

- Use your phone more and your legs less.
- Use your commuting time—for some, 1 to 4 hours each day.
- Time your job arrivals and departures.
- Train your [spouse] about trivial phone calls or office visits.
- Budget your time—analyze actual allocation to tasks.
- Don't become a slave to the clock.

CHAPTER 5
Scheduling Your Time

Scheduling expresses the divine pattern of time: *"God made time so that everything would not happen at the same time."* Scheduling may also help us as ministers do the best thing with our time, not just the most things. "Having the time of your life" includes developing skills and making time choices inside your life's total framework. So, six separate scheduling skills are organized into six topics, but each time-scheduling skill is both specific and synergistic. When you work with each skill as separate yet mutually

Planning and Time Management
Levels and scope of planning has much to do with the effective use of time.

Strategic Planning—5 to 10 years
Priority Planning—3 to 5 years
Operational Planning—1 to 2 years
Action Planning—1 to 12 months
Implementation—dly/wkly/mthly

© LEA, Inc.

dependent, your quality of life is more satisfying and ministry performance more rewarding. It makes it possible to do your scheduling from the large picture to the small components, and then back again. The same Lord who taught us to *"work for the night is coming"* also went often to be alone in spiritual retreat.

Schedules are important, but to paraphrase what Woody Allen once claimed: **"Showing up is 80% of life,"** and being on time helps. This chapter will help you refresh your skills and resources for significant short- and long-term planning. You may want to supplement this section with the support materials within other chapters. To contribute to personalizing your scheduling skills and planning, you can choose your own time pieces: computer, I-phone, Day Timer, pocket diary, watch and clock, current annual calendar, and multiyear planning calendar. (Note: If these are not adequate, turn to a good old trusty hour glass or sundial.)

GLOSSARY: "SCHEDULE"
from *The American Heritage® Dictionary*

Middle English "sedule," a slip of parchment or paper, a note; a list of times of departures and arrivals; a plan for performing work or achieving an objective, specifying the order and allotted time for each part; a printed or written list of items in tabular form; a program of events or appointments expected in a given time.

---

1. Strategic and Priority Planning—3 years to 10 years out

"Every moment spent planning saves three or four in execution" (from Crawford Greenwalt Dupont, 1972). From personal experience, I believe a 40- year old opinion is still about accurate. If you, your ministry leaders, and congregation are not already well ahead in the concept of Strategic Planning, consider these suggested actions:

- Set time frame: 5 to 10 years; at least 4 to 5 years.

- Include: dreaming, setting directions, personnel needs, church plant, community demographics, and other sea-changing issues.

⤳ Pursue "360 compass connections" for searching out possible directions.

⤳ Begin with biblical, strategic thinking about kingdom service.

⤳ Plan for and define your vision, values, and principles.

⤳ Involve the congregation in strategic time/ministry planning.

⤳ Focus on the mission/vision of the church.

⤳ Express objectives and goals of the church together.

⤳ Translate multiyear projects/activities into specific calendar dates.

⤳ Give priority to strategic time needs rather than operational calendars.

⤳ Keep a multiyear desk calendar for personal engagements and assignments.

⤳ Maintain records decisions and assignments for continuous work.

2. Annual Calendar Scheduling—12 months to 24 months out

Continue to make this function effective by drawing from the strategic planning and adding specifics, answering the age-old questions: Why? Who? What? When? Where? And, How? Working effectively at this time-skill is crucial because, ***"The Calendar doesn't care how you spend your time"***—(from Carlton Sheets, 12/20/87).

⤳ Show the "road map" of the major stops along the way; draw from your strategic planning, and the previous church calendars.

⤳ Operational planning is complete for next year; may include two years.

⤳ Face time with a larger number of lay leaders is often needed for effective planning, preparation, promotion and actual implementation.

⤳ Develop the church calendar with staff and lay leadership in the optimum time-cycles.

⤳ Balance calendar demands among the several church programs and ministries.

⤳ Coordinate calendar with regular communication and promotion.

~ Report the final annual to the congregation and relate it to the mission and priorities for that year.

~ Transfer related church dates to your own calendar.

~ Include your personal schedule: family vacation, holidays, personal engagements, professional development, etc.

~ Hang the "church calendar" on the wall and use the computer often; many times make it relevant to the life of the congregation.

3. Monthly Calendar Schedule and Update—3 to 4 weeks ahead

~ Review and update changes on the Annual Calendar.

~ Specific actions should be completely planned for implementation.

~ During the third or fourth week of each month, make a thorough review and update of next month's church calendar; with church staff, lay leaders, etc.

~ Review and update your personal calendar—write it down!

~ Compare the use of your time with the performance of your various functions.

~ Write time estimates into your calendar for preparation of major assignments, projects, meetings.

~ Prepare and/or maintain file folders for forthcoming assignments.

4. Weekly Schedule: Use Your Own Calendar Tools (at least by previous Friday)

~ Implementation is the key focus.

~ Start the week with reflection and planning—pen in hand.

~ Develop a weekly calendar and translate it into daily tasks and responsibilities.

~ Schedule a "weekly staff meeting" (even if it is a volunteer or part-time staff).

~ Include the required church meetings in your weekly schedule.

- Allocate time early in the week for sermon/worship/teaching preparation.

- Maintain an information/action file for that week's special events or projects.

- Early in the week, properly delegate assignments to team members.

- Designate a "day off" or "time off" and stick to it.

5. Daily Appointments: Your Daily Work Schedule

"How does a project get to be a year behind schedule? One day at a time." —Fred Brooks, IBM, chief designer. What habits already serve you well?

- Work with a pocket calendar, "Day Timer," computer, and desk calendar.

- Start each day with a personal quiet time with the Lord.

- Focus regularly on your mission and the church's "big picture."

- Develop appointment procedures, and assist the members to benefit by it.

- Use a standard appointment timeframe to be 15 minutes, and not 60!

- Delegate extensively and early in the work day.

- Schedule appointments an hour or more after the office day begins.

- Start on time, stay on time, stop on time.

- Do not allow interruptions, especially the telephone, during appointments.

- The clock is ticking; but don't let it overtake you.

6. "Do-It-Today" List—twelve proven practices

"Do it today list" is in fact self-management of your time and life. This list of a dozen practices for creating "to-do lists" grows out of years of practicing this discipline, poorly and with some success, and from published resources—such as Marshall J. Cook's <u>Time Management</u>, pp. 27-36. It could contribute to your taking continuous action on your priorities within a balanced schedule. Hopefully, it could also reduce your frustration. It is one tool to obey the injunction of our Lord **in John 9:4 –** *"As long as it is day, we must do the work of him who sent me. Night is coming, when no one can work."*

1. **Write a "must-do-today list," most, if not every day;** either in the previous evening or first thing in the morning. Use a smart phone, computer, or even a 3 x 5 card. But leave the listing behind you when you are on holiday with your family.

2. **Include known tasks, responsibilities, appointments, and essential prep time.** However, tell yourself and the list that it is just a tool—not your master or monster.

3. **Start with the most important things first; number them in order of priority.** Tackle hard tasks well before the end of the day; focusing on the important more than the urgent. Order the list creatively to take up high priorities before you drown in the small stuff.

4. **Break large tasks (boulders) into manageable size (pebbles).** Two hours a day for four days may be more reasonable than an eight-hour-day project.

5. **Group related ministry tasks and do them in a timely sequence.** Create a travel route for your visitation calls; block your study time for high performance; return phone calls or email during a between-time-period.

6. **Don't put too much on the list; jamming it with unreasonable expectations is a recipe for frustration.** Put some air in it; back-to-back scheduling may cause reduced performance.

7. **If your list involves work with others, set that out early enough to fit into "their lists."** Work together to truly serve the church's ministry as well as serve one another.

8. **Be realistic and allow for contingencies.** Don't carve the list on stone tablets— keep it flexible to fit your real time. Stand ready to chunk the list; something in your life—joy, sorrow, an opportunity—may become so much more important than "the list."

9. **Keep it personal—schedule some breaks, time-out time, and reward time;** keep your days and your life balanced.

10. **Balance your personal and strategic objectives as well as the daily goals/ tasks.** "What's scheduled usually gets done."

11. **You don't have to make a list every day—or in the same way, or at all;** make sure it serves you. Cross off completed tasks from the list. Revise and add to the list as needed.

12. **Remember to include your personal and family priorities on your daily "to-do" list;** that's when the list enriches the family members and helps to balance your life.

Chapter Conclusion/Reflection—The $25,000 Question

Among the six time-scheduling strategies: Where are you the strongest in time scheduling? Which strategy do you need most to improve? What actions will you take? It is my hunch that practicing the discipline of the "to do list" might offer the most immediate benefit as a frontend action. Take to heart the story of one of the earliest time management consultants:

The $25,000 Question has been reported in many publications, apparently first in The Time Trap by Alec MacKenzie, 1972.

The usefulness of planning a day's work is seen in a well-known story about Charles Schwab (1880-1939). When he was president of Bethlehem Steel, he presented this challenge to Ivy Lee, a consultant: "Show me a way to get more things done with my time, and I'll pay you any fee within reason."

Handing Schwab a piece of paper, Lee said, "Write down the most important tasks you have to do tomorrow and number them in order of importance. When you arrive in the morning, begin at once on No. 1 and stay on it till it's completed. Recheck you priorities; then begin with No. 2. If any task takes all day, never mind. Stick with it as long as it's the most important one. If you don't finish them all, you probably couldn't do so with any other method. Make this a habit every working day. When it works for you, give it to your men. Try it as long as you like. Then send me your check for what you think it's worth."

Some weeks later, Schwab sent Lee a check for $25,000 with a note saying that the lesson was the most profitable he had ever learned. In five years this plan was largely responsible for turning Bethlehem Steel Corporation into the biggest independent steel producer in the world.

Study Abstract by Lloyd Elder from Section One of:

"THE CLOCK AND THE COMPASS," <u>FIRST THINGS FIRST</u>
by Stephen R. Covey
A Fireside Book, New York: Simon & Schuster, 1995 (373 pages)

Stephen Covey starts by asking the question, *"If you were to pause and think seriously about the 'first things' in your life—the three or four things that matter most—what would they be?"* (p. 11). One of his strongest strategies to help answer this question is the analogy of the clock and the compass. The clock represents our commitments, appointments, schedules, goals, activities—what we do with and how we manage our time. The compass represents our vision, values, principles, mission, conscience, direction—what we feel is important and how we lead our lives (p. 19).

In an effort to close the gap between the clock and the compass, Covey turns to the field of "time management." He introduces the concept of what could be called the three "generations" of time management (pp. 21-22). Each generation builds on the one before it and moves toward greater efficiency and control, even toward a fourth generation. As a Christian minister, which generation is dominant in your life? All three have contributions to make.

First Generation. The first generation is based on "reminders." It's "go with the flow," but try to keep track of things you want to do with your time—write the report, attend the meeting, fix the car, clean out the garage. This generation is characterized by simple notes and checklists. If you're in this generation, you carry these lists with you and refer to them so you don't forget to do things. Hopefully, at the end of the day, you've accomplished many of the things that you set out to do and you can check them off your list. If those tasks are not accomplished, you put them on your list for tomorrow.

Second Generation. The second generation is one of "planning and preparation." It's characterized by calendars and appointment books. It pursues efficiency, personal responsibility, and achievement in goal setting, planning ahead, and scheduling future activities and events. If you're in this generation, you make appointments, write down commitments, identify deadlines, and note where meetings will be held. You may even keep this in some kind of computer or network.

Third Generation. The third generation approach is "planning, prioritizing, and controlling." If you're in this generation, you've probably spent some time clarifying your values and priorities. You've asked yourself, "What do I want?" You've set long-, medium-, and short-range goals to obtain these values. You prioritize your activities on a daily basis. This generation is characterized by a wide variety of planners and organizers—electronic as well as paper-based—with detailed forms for daily planning.

CHAPTER 6
Overcoming Time-Wasters

TIME TO FOCUS

None other than **the renowned Benjamin Franklin** left us his thoughts on this topic: *"Dost thou love life? Then do not squander time, for it is the stuff life is made of."*

Taking Charge

We must consider time management strategies to deal with "time-wasters." For all of those powerful planning ideas, scheduling actions, note-taking, and to-do lists, one of the critical enemies of good time management is "time-wasters." Time-wasters are the contenders for your limited time, habits that take charge of your best intentions, well-meaning associates willing to share in your comic relief, or even the good chosen instead of the best you have. Like everyone, you have your own danger spots that can eat up chunks of valuable time before you know it. The purpose of this chapter may seem to be quite negative, but not so. Rather it intends to help you identify 15 of the most common time-wasters threatening your life and work. But it will also present some helpful strategies for overcoming your time-wasters and taking charge of your time!

Believe it or not, you are not alone! Leaders from all professions are burdened with time-wasters. The purpose intended here is to enable you to think about your own work and life situation, to create your own list of common pitfalls. Our practical suggestions are offered, hopefully, in keeping with the passionate encouragement of Jesus to His followers: ***"As long as it is day, we must do the work of him who sent me. Night is coming, when no one can work."***—John 9:4

Reflection: Included here from research and experiences (some good and quite a few pitiful) is a list of common time-wasting practices. For each one that applies to you, read carefully the description, along with proven strategies for confronting that "waster." After you've done that and pondered your specific interest, write down or underline your own thoughts and plans for action.

Procrastination, the Chief Time-Thief

"Procrastination is the thief of time. Collar him!"—asserts none other than Charles Dickens. Contemporary surveys and authorities have found that "procrastination" is often at the head of the lists of all time-wasters. Procrastination takes several forms, such as: 1) Mental, "I'm still thinking about that." 2) Feeling: "I'm afraid I won't do it right." 3) Planning: "I know I said I would do it today, but I am still developing my way to go about it." 4) Physical: frantic action after it's too late.

Procrastination finds its way into the practice of almost every other common time-waster. You can find its place at the table when you sit down to serve up your dish to be tasted. Consider these artful ways of procrastination as it has been described:

- Procrastination is the practice of *"putting off doing something, especially out of habitual carelessness or laziness; to postpone or to delay needlessly."* (from Dictionary.com)

- *"Why do you wait, dear brother, Oh, why do you tarry so long?"* Could not this be called the theme song of all procrastinators? Acting on faith in Christ has a most critical life consequence.

- *"I'm going to stop putting things off; starting tomorrow."*

- *"Procrastination is the art of keeping up with yesterday."* (Don Marquis)

- *"Thank God for 'the last minute'; otherwise, nothing would ever get done."*

- *"He slept beneath the moon, he basked beneath the sun; He lived a life of 'going-to-do,' and died with nothing done."* (James Albery, 1838-1889)

Skills and Practices for Procrastination

- Most of the practices in the following 15 time-wasters will apply to practice of and solutions for procrastination; pay close attention to those that matter to you.

- Know what it takes to achieve your mission, pursue your priorities, and balance your life.

- Plan your work and work your plan; to know what you should do is only the first step.

- Focus on the positive, on moving forward: keeping your promises, not preparing apologies.

- Develop new skills and pattern of action into your behavior; be results oriented.

- Live out intentionally and with high priority your personal and family life.

- **Now, let's begin to treat fifteen time-wasters, describing the problem and proposing solutions.**

1. **Trivial Pursuits:** Inessential activities that promote none of the life purpose and need for balance you have set out for yourself. Trivial pursuits become procrastination by meaningless activity such as daydreaming, television, surfing the computer, curiosity born of sensationalism, etc. **Skills/Practices:**

   ❖ "Keep your eyes on the prize"—prioritize every day, not just January 1.

   ❖ If an insignificant activity brings you pleasure, use it to reward yourself for constructive things completed.

❖ Limit your time for obvious trivia; do so ahead of time!

❖ Keep a list of true priorities that often get neglected—family, friends, etc.; because saying you "never have the time" doesn't resolve the issue.

2. **Lack of Focus:** *"We always have time enough, if we but use it aright."* (from Goethe, 1749-1832) Examples: straying from the planned path; detours and distractions. If you've ever let a stray piece of mail or unscheduled conversation lead you on an investigation that lasts all day, then you may be suffering from lack of focus! **Skills/Practices:**

❖ Believe in your priorities! Reaffirm the importance of your schedule and your organizing principles every day.

❖ Be organized! If you already have time set aside for pursuing correspondence, or tackling that peripheral issue, it can't distract you in the meantime.

❖ Take regular breaks and lunch to get away—give your mind a chance to stay fresh.

3. **Mistakes:** Hey, everyone makes mistakes, right? But mistakes can become time-wasters if they become a pattern, if they're needless or if you don't learn from them. Wrong turns aren't always avoidable, but they may take up just as much time as detours. **Skills/Practices:**

❖ Was this something you were qualified to be doing anyway? Delegate, delegate, delegate. Trust your staff—they might know more about some things than we do.

❖ Ask for help. How much time have you wasted out of pride because you didn't want to ask for help?

❖ Are you prepared? Prep time can minimize errors.

❖ Budget more time. Rushing creates errors all by itself.

4. **Aimless Associates:** You know the guy/gal … always seems to have time to stop in your office for lengthy chats, while you can't find the time to turn around with all you've got to do. **Skills/Practices:**

   ❖ Learn to keep the door nearly closed when you most need it; if they ask for just a couple of minutes, then don't sit down and get comfortable.

   ❖ If you're swamped at the moment, say so, and make a later appointment.

   ❖ Have someone else answer the phone if possible—and teach the phone answerer when to take messages rather than interrupt.

5. **Failure to Delegate:** When you find yourself doing everything; projects developing only one step at a time because you're needed at every level. **Skills/Practices:**

   ❖ Trust your staff/colleagues. It will empower them and free you.

   ❖ Make conscious decisions to involve other team members. There is nothing noble in doing it all yourself if in the end fewer things get done, and the people you work with do not grow.

   ❖ Have a procedure in place for instruction, report back, then appraisal. In between, stay out of the way!

   ❖ Avoid upward delegation, that is, someone passes their work to do because "you are so much better at it than I am."

6. **Pointless Meetings:** Do you maintain regularly scheduled meetings, even if there's nothing to accomplish? Do you attend meetings, even if your presence is not required? Pointless meetings can be huge time-wasters! **Skills/Practices:**

   ❖ Have a procedure in place for setting the agenda.

   ❖ If the deadline passes and the agenda is still empty, cancel the meeting!

   ❖ Start and stop meetings on time—don't encourage time-wasting during a meeting by indulging it!

❖ Make sure everyone who is necessary for an agenda item is available and prepared, or you may have to go over it again next week.

7. **Random Phone Calls:** The random phone caller expects you to be ready to talk— for business or for leisure—any time of the day, for as long as the caller would like. Needless to say, this isn't possible and can waste a lot of time! **Skills/Practices:**

❖ Remember, some seemingly random calls are, in fact, significant.

❖ "Train" a phone answerer about your availability to take random calls. If there is no phone answerer, get an answering machine and/or caller ID and "train" yourself to use it wisely! (I would do that during dinner, regularly)

❖ Make sure others are equipped to answer basic questions; this may eliminate half of your random calls.

❖ Schedule time for call-backs. Causing even random callers to try endlessly to catch you isn't helpful, or courteous.

8. **E-Mail and messaging:** Are you besieged by unwanted e-mail and friendly messaging? Do you check for new e-mail or messages every 60 seconds? Wasn't this technology supposed to conserve time, not waste it? **Skills/Practices:**

❖ Don't subscribe to lists you're only peripherally interested in, especially not from your office e-mail address. Subscriber lists are for sale and will multiply!

❖ Set a time for checking new mail and messages—more than once a day, but less than 40! Constant availability may keep you in touch but it will distract your focus from other important activities.

❖ "Spam to others" as you would have them "spam to you."

9. **Fear of Failure:** A common reason for procrastination, fear of failure will force you to push aside starting a project or task, and may keep you from finishing. **Skills/ Practices:**

❖ Remember your priorities, prepare yourself, and jump right in!

❖ Trust yourself: your abilities, self-awareness, and the support structure that trusted you enough to give you this responsibility to begin with.

❖ Make yourself get started and build your confidence. Set a projected time to start. Remember: The Lord is your Shepherd. You shall not want … He restores your soul … You will fear no evil, for He is with you. (Psalm 23)

10. **Overwhelmed:** Too much to do, too little time. Sometimes the sheer magnitude of work left to do can leave you paralyzed from doing any of it. And the more time you're distracted by all the other things that must be done, the less you're focused on the task at hand. **Skills/Practices:**

❖ Discuss the conflict of priorities with the one who makes assignments to you.

❖ Reassess your priorities and daily activities at regular intervals during the day. As events unfold, make realistic determinations of what can and can't be done.

❖ Delegate, delegate, delegate.

❖ Remember the mission! Evaluate your functions and activities as opportunities to further it, not to be an obstacle!

11. **Pleasure comes first:** Do you look at your do-it list and jump right to the most pleasurable things first? Just because your diet affords a piece of chocolate cake doesn't mean it's smart to eat it first! The same is true of your work schedule! **Skills/Practices:**

❖ Use pleasurable items as reward and incentive, or as a break during a more stressful work period.

❖ Make those tough phone calls and address those complex interpersonal issues early in the day. Everyone involved will be fresher, and that confrontational dread will be behind you for the rest of the day.

12. **Nibbling at the edges:** procrastination by getting the easy, peripheral elements of a project out of the way first. Do you find yourself dwelling on the simple elements of a task? The easy things sure can waste a lot of time if you're using them to put off the meat of the work. **Skills/Practices:**

   ❖ Get started, jump right in! You can only clear your desk so long, "just getting ready."

   ❖ Make your prioritized **to-do lists** detailed. Consciously decide to tackle the heart of an issue from the beginning. Intersperse the tough things with the simpler things throughout the day to give your stress level a break, but focus on, and prioritize the meaty things first.

13. **Designed Distractions:** Let's face it, we may be talking about TV here! Along with some Internet surfing, and two-hour lunch breaks. The consensus of most surveys indicate that the average American watches more than 4 hours of TV a day … that's 2 months a year, and 12 years of TV watching in a 72-year life. **Skills/Practices:**

   ❖ Remember your truest priorities. Do you spend more time on television and other designed distractions than you do on relationships with family and friends?

   ❖ Television in the workroom? Up to you if it is for a special occasion.

   ❖ Do not allow distractions during the work day to force you to work at family time.

   ❖ Arrive at work early to handle Internet reading needs.

   ❖ Make use of the commute: listen to news on the way, or to music, or even the Bible.

14. **Indecision:** By its very nature, indecision is a primary time-waster and a contributor to the procrastination habit. The causes: failure to focus, lack of courage, fear of risking, too little information, too much information, lack of systemic thinking in a complex decision, or too much concern for small decisions. **Skills/Practices:**

   ❖ Develop your decision-making process/style.

❖ Get focused on your priorities.

❖ If you are responsible for the decision, then you must consider the risk and act accordingly.

❖ Gather pertinent information, but only essential to a sound decision; do not collect "miscellaneous stuff."

❖ Develop decision options and evaluate each one of them.

❖ Decide on the best available option—and act. Do something.

❖ If it is a small decision, give yourself a short time limit.

15. **Laziness:** Now we've finally come to the bad "L" word: lazy—indolent, sluggish, slothful, easygoing. By whatever descriptive term, laziness wastes time, and leads to many of the previously stated behavior patterns. Also, it requires many of the other over-coming strategies. **Skills/Practices:**

❖ Some accusations are simply false and not founded on accurate information.

❖ Make a tough-minded inventory of your mental vigor and behavior patterns.

❖ Establish clear ministry/life/work priorities; improve your skill levels.

❖ Develop reasonable work habits.

❖ Focus, decide, act, log, assess—until the direction is an upward cycle.

Conclusion

There are really two parallel tracks for "overcoming your time-wasters:" 1st identify them and own them as your own; and 2nd establish a pattern of skills and practices that stand in the gap for you. Are you relatively free from time-wasting practices? If your answer is "Yes," then enjoy the affirmation and keep it up. If your answer is "No," then pick a specific starting place and engage in the battle for wiser, more satisfactory time and life management. You are the one to decide what matters most to you; plan what to do and gain a victory over time-wasters.

CHAPTER 7
Taking Charge of Your Ministry Time

M inistry, as the gift of God to the church, deserves our highest and best, including **taking charge of the time given to every calling and role in our ministry**. That is what we have come to in this closing chapter: to apply the principles and practices of time management. To do so is to stand in the very stream of biblical understanding:

> *It was he who gave some to be apostles, some to be prophets, some to be evangelists, and some to be pastors and teachers, to prepare God's people for works of service, so that the body of Christ may be built up ...* (Ephesians 4:11-12 NIV).

> *Do your best to present yourself to God as one approved, a workman who does not need to be ashamed and who correctly handles the word of truth. (2 Tim. 2:15)*

As a church leader, your most important time management need may be in preparation for worship and ministry. However, it also requires ministry time to care for others, participate in church meetings, office administration, relationship building, community/ mission projects, and a host of other services. How can it all get done? Good question. Developing time-management skills is a large step toward practicing servant leadership. By it, you set an **example** for others, you follow **ethical** motivation, you **equip** others for their tasks, you **effectively** transform activity into mission, and you become more **efficient** in your own ministry assignments.

Offered here are basic time practices for any minister and only five selected ministry functions for making the most of your time. Nurture expectations that any time reclaimed from the "not-important," could be reallocated as more time devoted to the "important." The goal is not simply to increase the quantity of work, but more so to enjoy satisfying quality and balance of life including family, personal, service to others, and, of course, your ministry position! Sometimes a few basic steps can keep you from repeating the same tasks each week, so let's start with the basic practices:

1st Framing the Larger Picture

First, let's reach back into the basics of time management and apply them to the practice of ministry:

- Seek to understand the biblical meaning of time for ministry.

- Inventory exactly what happens to your work time.

- Develop your ministry plan on the three principles of purpose, balance, and priority.

- Include in specific time-use planning the three practices of performance zone, consolidation, and pacing.

- Schedule your ministry time effectively; avoid time-wasters.

- These should lead to several "good time habits" throughout the study.

2nd Establishing Your Ministry Time Plan

- Consolidate your ministry tasks which may come to you in several ways: from your formal position description or expectations—assumed if not written; and assignments that have become permanent.

- Now make a list of these tasks, combining them into functions or categories. The listing in chapter 3 will serve as a starting place, but work on it until you have a customized list that fits you.

⁓ Assign to each ministry function a level of priority using a simple 1, 2, 3—1 low, 2 mid, 3 high priority. Priority should represent the relationship that function, or set of tasks, has to the mission of the church.

⁓ Establish a reasonable (required, actual, average) number of total ministry work hours per week for each ministry function; should not exceed the total hours of your expected workweek. Of your 40- to 48-hour ministry workweek, do you spend a major amount of that time on high priority?

3rd Practicing Good Time Habits

If you generally practice good, commonsense time habits, it will assist you in every area of ministry. Try some of these. They have proven helpful to my ministry and to others from whom I have learned.

⁓ Arrive 30 minutes early—especially if it gives you a better slot in the traffic pattern; or provides you a quiet time before the office storm breaks.

⁓ Leave 30 minutes late—if it gives you a break in the traffic, but also if it provides you time to "debrief," to read, or to write your "to-do" list for tomorrow.

⁓ Have materials with you so that you can read, or write, or listen, (instead of fume) while you wait; not everyone is going to be on your timeline.

⁓ Change your pace or task at selected intervals; do not wear yourself down against a temporary block, or simply move on to some trivial activity.

⁓ Use longer time frames for more demanding, priority tasks; use "short time for short stuff."

⁓ Seize the moment: concentrate on the task at hand, the problem before it becomes a crisis; and claim the opportunity while you can.

4th Time for Preaching/Teaching Preparation

"Be prepared" could be a helpful watchword for those of us in Christian ministry. The Apostle Paul wrote to his young associate, Timothy: ***Preach the word; be prepared in season and out of season; correct, rebuke, and encourage—with great patience and***

careful instruction (2 Tim. 4:2 NIV). The following are some "time-use" preparation suggestions for you to consider:

- Silence, prayer, and study are basic disciplines that enrich all preparation.

- Treat preparation for preaching, worship, and teaching as a firm, scheduled study appointment. Your congregation, whether 50 or 500 members, depends on you to be fully prepared. In truth, devout preparing is a meeting with the Almighty before you meet with the people.

- Plan your preaching ahead of time—by the month, quarter, season, or even a full year; such periodic planning maximizes your use of time.

- Bunch your study into blocks of time, (two or more hours) and as early in the week as possible. A periodic "sabbatical study" is great time economy in your calendar schedule.

- Request qualified members to do assigned research that you may fashion into the sermon to be preached; this could also include a reminder of related music, poetry, or art work.

- Keep a "sermon need and seed" file in a notebook, file drawer, shoe box, or computer.

- Include in your study computer resources: bible translations, concordances, dictionaries, commentaries, etc. (see our Bibliography/Web Links for selected study links).

- Follow a sermon series to conserve time and to enrich your preaching and teaching; a series may include: Bible book, Bible biographies, doctrinal, devotional, thematic, social issues, topical, etc. Preparation for several sermons at a time provides multiple use of background study.

- Maintain a "completed sermon" file so that you can readily retrieve, refresh, and reuse for other preaching assignments.

- Develop basic sermon/lesson worksheets; see sample worksheet and revise or expand to fit your need and style.

SAMPLE SERMON WORKSHEET

(Edit this and use it to organize each sermon)

Preaching Text:_____

Sermon Subject: (1-3 words)_____

Sermon Title:_____

Central Idea of the text: what does the text say?_____

_____

_____

_____

Sermon in a sentence: what does the sermon intend to communicate?_____

_____

_____

Major objective of the sermon: discipleship, grace, love, stewardship, etc._____

_____

What do you want others to be or to do?_____

_____

_____

SAMPLE SERMON STRUCTURE
(Edit this and use it to organize each sermon)

Sermon Title:_____

Sermon Text:_____

Introduction: (several paragraphs) *text, textual background, illustration, human need, etc.*_____

_____

_____

Body of the sermon: (Each point represents two pages/5-6 minutes each.) *The sermon should usually be developed by exposition of the text, illustration, argument from other texts or experience, application; may also use story form, question and answer, etc.*

Point I._____

_____

Point II._____

_____

Point III._____

_____

Develop other points as needed; usually not more than 4 or 5 points.

Conclusion: (a few paragraphs, two minutes or so; this could include the invitation)_____

_____

_____

Invitation: (brief, specific appeal based on, or implied by the sermon)_____

_____

_____

5th Time for Church or Ministry Team Meetings

Develop a standard format for planning meetings and agendas. Example:

Group: Deacons Meeting

Agenda: Prepared by chairperson, with pastor

Date: for Monday, March 4, 2013

Time: Start—7:00 p.m.; Close—8:30 p.m.

Place: Church Fellowship Hall

Notices: By church office on Feb 21, 2013

Tips for Meetings: these actions conserve valuable time and contribute to a purposeful outcome and full member participation. **Reflection:** How could these suggestions apply for one of your own specific meetings?

- Determine the purpose of the meeting and who should be present.
- Send notices and reminders about the meeting.
- Prepare and distribute agenda, with time estimates for items. (Be sure members know regular procedure for getting items on the agenda.)
- Secure needed room, equipment/supplies (delegate this!).
- Prepare and provide printed reports and materials.
- Start on time, stay on agenda, and stop on time.
- Provide time for team-building and skill development.
- Follow orderly discussion and have standard procedures in place for decision-making, brainstorming, team-building, planning, or_____.
- Make clear follow-up assignments.
- Record accurate minutes and distribute them after the meeting.
- **Cancel pointless meetings before they happen.**

6th Time for Office Administration

Answering the Phone: a primary communication link:

- Train the secretary/volunteer or yourself: "not available, may I help you?"

- Save yourself the phone tag—know which calls to take now.

- Use answering machine/voice mail unless the message content requires direct voice response.

- Bunch your return calls, but at a time you might get through.

- Plan for short, clear phone conversations.

- Make notes of what you need to communicate clearly; May even ask, "Do you have a pen in hand?"

- Take notes on the conversation, especially the business side of the whole.

- Follow up with essential hard copy or e-mail.

- "Let your fingers do the walking"—call hospital patients, members, guests, vendors to confirm availability.

Making/Keeping Appointments: meeting with others

- Whose responsibility is it to schedule your appointments?

- Have a set procedure in place so that you do not confuse the schedule.

- Group your appointments so that you can create blocks of time for other tasks.

- Establish starting and stopping times up-front: "I can meet from … until …"

- Be prepared for appointments: talking points, proposals, facts, details, reports, budget, calendar, or whatever is needed.

Opening the Mail/E-Mail:

- Block off times to process mail, e-mail, and phone texting.

- Handle mail only once, and in short timeframes.

- Learn to make quick "save it" or "trash it" decisions on the spot; if it has to wait, have a holding tray, or put in the appropriate file.

- Scribble/type brief, personal responses on an original letter or report; this is becoming more acceptable. "OK, go with this and let's talk Friday." Keep a copy if you need a record (that's how the e-mail works).

- Respond by phone when possible—when discussion is needed or additional options considered; keep it focused and brief.

- Refer correspondence to the appropriate person. Don't try to make all the connections yourself!

- Remove yourself from every mail or e-mail list that is unnecessary. Junk e-mail wastes time.

7th Time for Working with People

- Get training for staff supervision, if it is a major function.

- Close your door (partly) when you need to; create a two-sided sign—"Quiet Work Time" or "Knock & Come Right In."

- Set blocks of time for projects and preparation.

- For a short work meeting, you stop by the other person's office.

- Make appointments only for time needed for the business: starting and stopping times really help; think in 15 to 20 minute segments.

- Stay connected, but be careful about the two-hour luncheon or the 30-minute coffee break.

- Don't waste the time of your team members, or yours.

- Learn to say "No." Remember the mission, the life-balance, and the commitment to things that will get you there. If there's something you can do, start your rejection with the positive: "I can come and sit in on the last half of your meeting, but I won't be available to plan and lead the discussion."

- Get to work on your "Yes." Chances are, your plate is full of obligations to others—get to it in a timely fashion!

- Recognize when a project is "dead" and let it go. Don't waste time trying to "rescue the perishing" if its usefulness is already gone.

- Delegate, delegate, delegate. Perhaps the most important single leadership skill for time management is delegation.

Time for Delegation

Delegation frees up time for the leader and empowers the other team members! It is an essential act of leadership for both the time saved in the short run and the great unknown things that may be done in the future as your staff begins to claim ownership in the ministry. Delegation enhances the possibility that "my ministry" will become "our ministry" at the same time that your leadership can spend more time on the overall vision. Important elements of delegation:

- **Selection**—Choose a team member whose skills and availability match the task in question. Arbitrary rotation of assignments may be just poor management, not leadership!

- **Direction**—Make directions clear and full of optimistic encouragement. Expect of the receiving team member as high a standard of excellence as you would of yourself.

- **Observation**—Stay out of the way! Establish trust with the delegate. Provide necessary access and resources. Be clear about deadlines and update intervals.

- **Control**—Let go. It's ok if the project in question develops in a way that is not identical to the way you would have developed it. Allow the persons you have selected to be themselves, and utilize their own strengths and perspectives when possible.

- **Appraisal**—Be honest and encouraging. Listen! Reward completed tasks; learn from mistakes and write it down.

8th Time for Ministry Projects

How do you keep your ministry projects moving forward with confidence? The following will serve as a checklist of project components.

- Define the project early, clearly, and succinctly; use the "six stalwart questions" as a guide:

  - What is going to be done?

  - Why are we going to do this?

  - Who is going to be served?

  - Where is the location, places of the project?

  - When is the project going to begin and end?

  - How are we going to work together to accomplish the task(s)?

- Establish a planning team involving essential persons:

  - Responsibility persons for the team and within the team

  - Skill/support persons or groups based on the nature of the project

  - Participants/constituents/members/community volunteers

  - Other?

- Outline the project phases and steps:

  - Planning

  - Implementation

  - Approval

  - Completion

  - Preparation

  - Evaluation

- Delegate Responsibilities/Functions:

  - Program/leadership

  - Promotion/communication

  - Financial support

  - Scheduling/calendar

  - Physical support

- Evaluation/Assessment: Take time to assess the project by its designed objectives.

A TIMELY REFLECTION ON
TAKING CHARGE OF YOUR TIME
[from an unknown source]

One day an expert was speaking to a group of business students about time management. He pulled out a one-gallon, wide-mouthed Mason jar and set it on a table in front of him. Then he produced about a dozen fist-sized rocks and carefully placed them, one at a time, into the jar. When the jar was filled to the top and no more rocks would fit inside, he asked, "Is this jar full?" Everyone in the class said, "Yes."

Then he said, "Really?" He reached under the table and pulled out a bucket of gravel. Then he dumped some gravel in and shook the jar, causing pieces of gravel to work themselves down into the spaces between the big rocks. Then he asked the group once more, "Is the jar full?"

By this time the class was onto him. "Probably not," one of them answered. "Good!" he replied. He reached under the table and brought out a bucket of sand. He started dumping the sand in, and it went into all the spaces left between the rocks and the gravel. Once more he asked the question, "Is this jar full?" "No!" the class shouted. Once again he said, "Good!"

Then he grabbed a pitcher of water and began to pour it in until the jar was filled to the brim. Then he looked up at the class and asked, "What is the point of this illustration?"

One student raised their hand and said, "The point is, no matter how full your schedule is, if you try really hard, you can always fit some more things into it!" "No," the speaker replied, "that's not the point. The truth this illustration teaches us is, if you don't put the big rocks in first, you'll never get them in at all."

Reflection

I want my jar full when it's time to go to the other side of my life. But for now, "I'm having the time of my life!"

PART 2

TAKING CHARGE OF YOUR STRESS:
"For the Sake of Life and Ministry"

CHAPTER 8
Taking Charge of Your Stress for Your Own Sake

PART 2 OBJECTIVE

To advance proven skills for managing stress in Christian ministry and everyday living:

1) **by exploring ways to understand stress and its causes;**

2) **by examining practices to guard against excessive stress and burnout in church life and ministry; and**

3) **by developing proven strategies for life-long coping with stress.**

1. Key Stress Matters: Starting at the Beginning

Stress Texts at the Start: In most bible translations, the term "stress" is not used, but the concept of stress is expressed in so many different words. At the outset of Part 2, "Taking Charge of Your Stress for Your Own Sake," let selected verses of Holy Scripture introduce the concept and locate you right in the middle of it:

Matthew 6:33-34—"*But seek first his kingdom and his righteousness, and all these things will be given to you as well. Therefore do not worry about* *tomorrow, for tomorrow will worry about itself. Each day has enough trouble of its own."*

John 16:33—*"I have told you these things, so that in me you may have peace. In this world you will have trouble [to be pressed down]. But take heart! I have overcome the world."*

2 Corinthians 4:8-9—*"We are hard pressed on every side, but not crushed; perplexed, but not in despair; persecuted, but not abandoned; struck down, but not destroyed."*

1 Peter 5:7—*"Cast all your anxiety on him because he cares for you."*

Contemporary Thoughts—Just a brief listen:

"Stress can be fantastic. Or it can be fatal. It's all up to you. As well as respecting the dangers of stress, you can learn to harness its benefits." (from The Joy of Stress by Dr. Peter Hanson)

"Don't let the alligators get you!" **Is this cartoon motto good for you and for others who have too many people or things in a tug-of-war in the swamp of your time and attention?** (from a SkillTrack® cartoon)

"It is better to bend than to break." (Aesop—a Greek fabulist, 620-560 B. C., not exactly our contemporary to us)

Popular Views:

We all have some basic ideas of what stress is, common sayings linked to stress, such as: **"on edge," "up tight," "under pressure," "at my wits end,"** and even **"bad hair day!"**

Stress—Short-Term/Long-Term:

Often we increase our skill in coping with stress by analyzing its duration; stress in personal, family, and ministry life. This is only a preliminary look at the pattern and duration of your stress. Let's keep it brief for now:

- **Short-term stress** may be like a "blip on the screen"—it's there and begs to be acknowledged but could be experienced, identified, and resolved in moments. Target the stress; don't let it submerge and bubble up later, such as: late for a staff meeting, severe headache, out of cash, heated words with salesperson, lost in a new neighborhood, etc.

- **Long-term stress** may be permanent or reoccurring and often severe; so it could be feared, avoided, or expected but requires intentional coping skills. Examples include: personal or business or family conflict, high blood pressure, maxed-out credit cards, trouble with personnel committee, schedule demands, etc.

Where do you fit in? The American Institute of Stress has recently reported: sixty to 90 percent of people seen in their primary care physician's office have symptoms or illnesses linked to stress and lifestyle choices. Seven out of 10 of the leading causes of death in the U.S. could be greatly reduced if lifestyle habits were modified, including poor or negative responses to stress and tension.

2. Taking Charge: Responsibility, Accountability, and Reliability

Is there a case for dealing with time and stress in the same text/workbook? Yes, and we have already done so, but let's walk through it again with stress on our mind:

- Because "taking charge of your stress" is your **responsibility**, your job; it is your **accountability** to live with the consequences; and it is the expectancy of others for you to consistently practice **reliability**, e.g. "you can count on me" relationships.

- Because "taking charge" of your stress is first and foremost in your life journey, the stress you generate, receive, and feel really matters. You can be able to take charge of what you know, what you think, what you decide, how you conduct yourself, and how you respond. Stress is most often in the responding, as often quipped:

> ***"It's not what happens to you,***
> ***but what you do with what happens to you."***

- Because managing your stress and doing it well is first for your own sake; this is your life you are living in, so you are not doing it just to impress another or because someone demands it of you. Your stress can't be managed around the water cooler, by a third party, or at a pity party.

- Because this book is developed and designed to be a **text/workbook**—a resource that intends to provide spiritual, mental, emotional, and practical dimensions to the study of stress, but calls you into the process to do the work.

- Because in our research, experience, and testimony, we have found that so very often time and stress are better worked at together; that in 60% to 70% of our life experiences, good or bad, time and stress seem to travel together. They call for similar skill-sets and yet have unique baggage and issues to face.

What does it look like to stand inside of "taking charge of your stress?"

This chapter, and more completely developed throughout Part 2, seeks to strengthen your cognitive and assessment tools about stress and stress management. First we want to stand within our own life to see what "taking charge of stress" could be like if we enjoyed a certain set of skills and benefits:

- Having an open, life-long "conversation" about your stress management

- Listening for the voice of God in the midst of your life

- Becoming more reflective, quiet, and responsive

- Keeping your family in the big picture; the main thing as the main thing

- Developing genuine autonomy and significance as a person

- Accepting the value and autonomy of those around you

- Living a whole and balanced life; even good things may get you out of whack

- Taking charge of your life's direction and intentions with purpose

- Transforming your external landscape; "courage to change what can be changed"

- Improving your ministry performance and productivity

- Staying put in your ministry, with satisfaction and vision

- Contributing to your spiritual, mental, social, and physical health

3. Introducing Stress Definitions and Response Skill-Sets

❖ **Definitions: Looking Under the Surface:** Our examination of definitions and basic truths about stress is like looking under the surface of stress in order to understand its makeup and then to develop useful skills to respond in appropriate and healthy ways. This brief introduction here will be more carefully developed chapter by chapter, adding scores of skills and practices for life and leadership. For now, begin with one definition, followed by a number of characteristics of "stress."

GLOSSARY: "STRESS"
from *Strength for the Journey*, by Porowski and Carlisle,
Nashville TN, LifeWay Press. p. 110

Stress is a person's response to overload, the accumulation effect of the pressures of life. Daily tasks, job-related duties and volunteer projects may not appear staggering when viewed individually, but when they begin to layer one upon another, they can reach overwhelming proportions.

- Stress is the buildup of pressure on the outside that makes you feel tense on the inside.

- Stress always involves both outside stimuli (stressors) effecting us and internal responses by us.

- Stress is your body sending signals that your physical or emotional well-being feels threatened.

- Stress is the body's "alarm system" activating its defense system.

- Stress is unavoidable in life, and is indeed a necessary sign of life.

⤳ Stress is not all bad; it can be essential to life.

⤳ Stress is a fact of life—stimulating, motivating, challenging.

⤳ Excess stress can make you unproductive, miserable, unsure, fearful, and even ill.

Reflection: What are your own thoughts about stress that you want to explore as you work at taking charge of your stress?

✤ **Framework: Stress Response Skill-Sets**

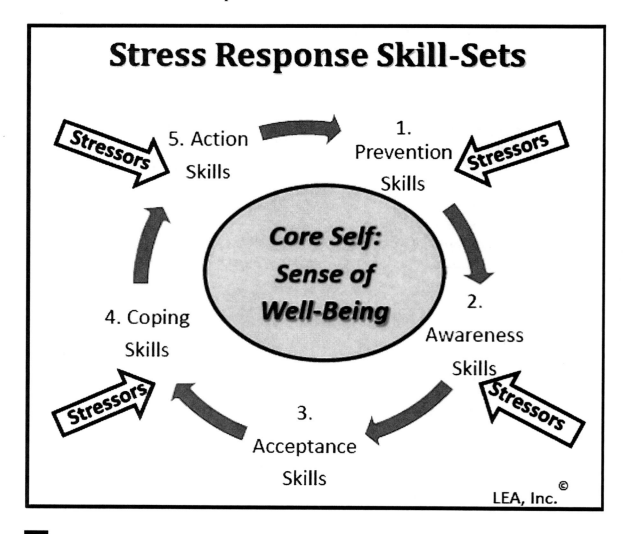

Stress Response Skill-Sets

5. Action Skills

1. Prevention Skills

Core Self: Sense of Well-Being

2. Awareness Skills

4. Coping Skills

3. Acceptance Skills

Stressors

Stressors

Stressors

Stressors

LEA, Inc. ©

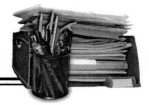

The objective of **Part 2: "Taking Charge of Stress: For the Sake of Your Life"** is to set out proven skills and best practices to handle stress in a healthy and productive manner. The graphic presented now seeks to focus on five response skill-sets that are explored throughout this seven-chapter treatment. Any graphic has its limitations; especially when static elements seek to symbolize human feelings and responses.

Let me summarize the major elements of the graphic:

- **Core Self—Sense of Well-Being**: each individual is a complex makeup of personal (self-image), mental (cognitive), emotional, social (value system), and physical characteristics; this also houses a certain "stress print" that may be defined as either helpful or harmful.

- **Stressors**: are the causes of stress those persons, events, conditions, etc., that pose a threat to one's sense of well-being.

- **Stress Response Skill-Sets:** there are five or more such sets of skills that may be utilized in the management of stress; also, scores of specific things to and actions to take within each set:

  1. **Prevention Skills:** skills that include developing a strong autonomy and self understanding; that confront the stressor on the front end and reject it as your reality; that resists and guards against accepting every stressor as your own.

  2. **Awareness Skills:** skills that help to sense that there is a threat to well-being, what causes the threat, and what can and should be done about it?

  3. **Acceptance Skills:** accepting stressors (causes) of stress that you cannot change, but that you may change your response to it; the stress may be real, even overwhelming, that it is yours to be accepted and cannot be ignored.

  4. **Coping Skills:** skills such as understanding stress,(cognitive), identify your stress feelings, assess the specific cause or stressor, singular or oft repeated, actions, handy toolbox of proven skills, professional or wise personal helpers.

  5. **Actions Skills:** stress that can be changed by actions that you may pursue, even developing to more positive behavior patterns.

4. What about You and the Whole Stress Scene?

In this overview chapter of stress management we are seeking to invite you into a look at the whole scene before us. Here is how we are seeking to make progress in an orderly but open fashion in four categories of interest to you.

- **Introducing stress management:** raises awareness of stress and understandings about its meaning in relationship to your life and leadership in ministry. A cartoon quip oversimplifies the whole matter: *"I feel much better now that I have given up all hope."* Do you ever feel like that? Anyway, we will report working understandings about stress and its effects on us.

- **Assessing causes of stress:** examines common causes of stress and identifies stress factors related directly to Christian ministry. A "stressor" is any phenomenon that triggers a stress response. This category will explore many of the stressors and stress issues that seem particular to those in ministry.

  "No matter how old you are, you always think that there may be something hiding under the bed." —Monica, age 13, from Youth Calendar

- **Guarding against stress:** establish practical ways to discover and to guard against excess stress, or burnout, in life and leadership. Burnout is the ultimate, downward spiraling result of ignored stress, like the condition of a car run for too long, too hard, and with too little coolant or maintenance.

- **Strategies for coping with stress:** develops and proposes sound practices and strategies to cope with ministry stress in a life-long, healthy manner. Ministers have unique outlets for managing the stresses that are particular to the work of church leaders, even to turn them into positives for your life and leadership.

  Philippians 4:6—"Do *not be anxious about anything, but in everything, by prayer and petition, with thanksgiving, present your requests to God.*"

> *"God grant me the serenity to accept the things I cannot change; courage to change the things I can; and wisdom to know the difference."* —attributed to Reinhold Niebuhr

SkillTrack® first published this material as a text curriculum for conference and independent study. It has been applauded by many in diverse audiences of Christian ministers to be effective in developing stress managers. We have the same reason for publishing the book including stress management, with very specific goals:

- to add to your understanding

- to guide your self-assessment

- to develop coping skills

- do diagnose ministry stressors

- to provide you a "toolbox"

- to call for action planning

- to use for lifetime growth

- to call on Christian resources

Why not study these chapters, why not post your thoughts about stress in your life and ministry. Just let your ideas flow like a video camera around your life. Then look for tools and benefits throughout the study.

5. Study Resource: "Symptoms of Anxiety: Three Categories"

This assessment resource, in the overview chapter of your "taking charge of stress," introduces you to one of many of the opportunities you have to call professionals into your own journey.

TAKING CHARGE of Your *Time* & *Stress*

A Study Abstract prepared by Lloyd Elder:

STUDY RESOURCE: "SYMPTOMS OF ANXIETY"

From an Internet article by Archibald D. Hart, Ph.D.
presented on http://www.troubledwith.com

Dr. Archibald reports that anxiety symptoms fall into three categories: physiological, cognitive, and emotional. If you count the following symptoms that apply to you, you may get an idea of your stress level. The checklist is designed to communicate a variety of symptoms; the more symptoms you experience, the more likely you may need to explore treatment for anxiety-related problems:

Physiological symptoms: What do you feel?

- Weak all over?
- Rapid, pounding heartbeat or palpitations?
- Tightness around your chest?
- Hyperventilation (a feeling that you cannot get enough air)?
- Periodic dizziness and sweating?
- Muscle tension, aches or tremors?
- Chronic fatigue?

Cognitive symptoms: What thoughts do you think?

- I can't carry on. I've got to get out of here.
- What if I make a fool of myself?
- People are looking at me all the time.
- I'm having a heart attack.
- I'm going to faint.
- I'm going crazy.
- I can't go on alone; no one will help me.
- I can't go out; I will lose control.
- I feel confused and can't remember things.

Emotional symptoms: How do you respond to yourself?

- I'm full of fears that I can't get out of my mind.
- I feel like something terrible is going to happen.
- I worry excessively.
- I feel uneasy and alone a lot of the time.
- I often feel isolated, lonely, down in the dumps and depressed.
- I feel I have no control over what happens to me.
- I feel embarrassed, rejected and criticized.
- I often feel like screaming with anger.

6. Study Resource: "101 Ways to Cope with Stress"

This following resource offered early in Part 2 introduces a large, practical list of acts and practices to cope with or prevent stress. It also covers personal and ministry arenas of stress causes and cures. These topics will be expanded throughout this study.

A Study Abstract prepared by Baptist Center for Health & Wellness:
STUDY RESOURCE: "101 WAYS TO COPE WITH STRESS"
Used by permission from
Baptist Center for Health & Wellness

• Get up 15 minutes earlier • Prepare for the morning the night before • Avoid tight fitting clothes • Avoid relying on chemical aids • Set appointments ahead • Don't rely on your memory … write it down • Practice preventative maintenance • Make duplicate keys • Say "NO" more often • Set priorities in your life • Avoid negative people • Use time wisely • Simplify meal times • Always make copies of important papers • Anticipate your needs • Repair anything that doesn't work properly • Ask for help with jobs you dislike • Break large tasks intro bite size portions • Look at problems as challenges • Look at challenges differently • Unclutter your life • Smile • Be prepared for rain • Tickle a baby • Pet a friendly dog/cat • Don't know all the answers • Look for the silver lining • Say something nice to someone • Teach a kid to fly a kite • Walk in the rain • Schedule play time into every day • Take a bubble bath • Be aware of the decisions you make • Believe in you • Stop saying negative things to yourself • Visualize yourself winning • Develop your sense of humor • Stop thinking tomorrow will be a better day • Have goals for yourself • Dance a jig • Say hello to a stranger • Ask a friend for a hug • Look up at the stars • Practice breathing slowly • Learn to whistle a tune • Read a poem • Listen to a symphony • Watch a ballet • Read a story curled up in bed • Do a brand new thing • Stop a bad habit • Buy yourself a flower • Take stock of your achievements • Find support from others • Ask someone to be your "vent-partner" • Do it today • Work at being cheerful and optimistic • Put safety first • Do everything in moderation • Pay attention to your appearance • Strive for excellence NOT perfection • Stretch your limits each day • Look at a work of art • Hum a jingle • Maintain a healthy weight • Plant a tree • Feed the birds • Practice grace under pressure • Stand up and stretch • Always have a plan "B" • Learn a new doodle • Memorize a joke • Be responsible for your feelings • Learn to meet your own needs • Become a better listener • Know your limitations and let others know them too • Tell someone to have a good day in pig latin • Throw a paper airplane • Exercise every day • Learn the works to a new song • Get to work early • Clean out a closet • Play patty cake with a toddler • Go on a picnic • Take a different route to work • Leave work early (with permission) • Put air freshener in your car • Watch a movie and eat popcorn • Write a note to a friend far away • Go to a ball game and scream • Cook a meal and eat it by candlelight • Recognize the importance of unconditional love • Give yourself permission to get professional help if you need it • Keep a journal • Practice a monster smile • Remember you always have options • Have a support network of people, places and things • Quit trying to "fix" other people • Get enough sleep • Talk less and listen more • Freely praise other people • P.S. Relax, take each day one at a time … you have the rest of your life to live.

CHAPTER 9
Understandings About This Thing Called Stress

1. Understandings about Stress: the Saga of the Rubber Bands

A s part of my understandings about stress, I want to relate a visual story about the "Rubber Band." Yes, I have actually demonstrated this in dozens of conferences on stress, not just as an "ice breaker" but as critical understandings about stress. I will provide only limited explanation about this parable. Rubber bands, like stress, have many functional qualities, such as: tasks, sizes, shapes, strengths, flexibility, durability, and limitations:

1. **The extremely large rubber band**: needs to be large enough for a specific task like my hip rehab regimen instead of hip surgery; but it is much too large for small tasks. So with large surges of stress.

2. **Many smaller rubber bands** may be just right for all sorts of ordinary uses in life and work; usually one chooses the size and strength to fit the task. So with stress.

3. **Hinders: A rubber band at rest "hinders" performance** in that it exists and is available for use, but in fact it is not doing any task that it was made to perform. To function without stress at all is to underperform by avoiding a valuable capacity for life and work. So with stress.

4. **Helps: A rubber band at work "helps"** because it exists, is available, and is used to perform one of the many tasks it is capable of doing. "Functional stress" helps us to function to our capacity.

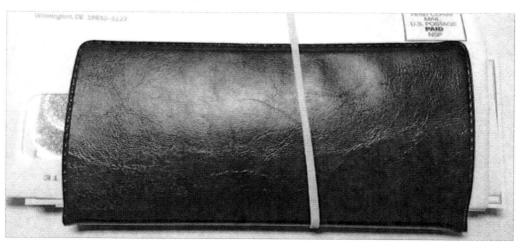

5. **Harms: A rubber band "stretched out"** is likely to deteriorate, or to hold until it breaks and then has no stretch at all (and when it pops it may well hurt). Much like dysfunctional stress.

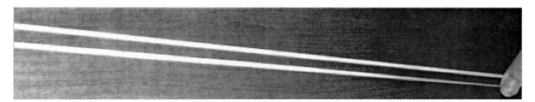

2. Learning about the Stress We Know

"Taking Charge of Your Stress" has as a foremost need a basic understanding of stress. This is not a theoretical search, but a sincere attempt to keep you in the picture and doing your own work. The purpose of this chapter is to raise your stress awareness and to understand its meaning in relationship to your life and leadership in ministry. You are encouraged to explore how you fit in.

❖ **Stress: Fitting into the Picture**

- **A key biblical text of encouragement is found in 1 Peter 5:7—*Cast all your anxiety* [stress] *on him because he cares for you.***

- Six centuries before Christ, Aesop the Greek fabulist is quoted as saying, ***"It is better to bend than to break."***

- Popular expressions: We all have some basic ideas of what stress is, even if specific in-depth definitions are a bit elusive. Popular sayings linked to stress are used all the time: "on edge," "up tight," "under pressure," at wit's end," "you're on my last nerve," even "bad hair day!"

❖ **Stress: Basic Truths**

- Understandings: Getting under the surface of stress to understand what it's introduced in Chapter 8, the following are significant components embedded in most definitions as a starting point.

  • Stress always involves both outside stimuli (stressors) effecting us and internal responses by us.

- Stress is your body sending signals that your physical or emotional well-being feels threatened.

- Stress is the body's "alarm system" activating its defense system.

- Stress is unavoidable in life, and is indeed a necessary sign of life.

- Stress is not all bad; it can be essential to life.

- Stress is a fact of life—stimulating, motivating, challenging.

- However, excess stress can make you unproductive, miserable, unsure, fearful, and even ill.

❖ Stress: Selected Definitions

With those things in mind, consider the following definitions—taken from various sources related to stress:

- *"Stress is the build-up of pressure on the outside that makes you feel tense on the inside. Some stress is a part of daily life—affects everyone. Certain kinds are actually helpful—they keep you on our toes. But too much stress on your mind and body can make you miserable—worried, sad and ill."* (from Scriptographic Booklet on Stress Management)

- *"Stress is a mind-body arousal that, on one hand, can save our lives, and on the other hand, can fatigue body systems to the point of malfunction and disease* (from <u>Controlling Stress and Tension</u>, p.1 by Daniel Girdano et al)

- *"Stress is a person's response to overload, the accumulation effect of the pressures of life. Daily tasks, job-related duties and volunteer projects may not appear staggering when viewed individually, but when they begin to layer one upon another, they can reach overwhelming proportions."* (from <u>Strength for the Journey</u>, p. 110)

- *"Stress is the psychological and physiological reaction that takes place when you perceive an imbalance in the level of demand placed on you and your*

capacity to meet that demand."—The Complete Idiot's Guide to Managing Stress, p. 19 (Don't let this title "stress you out.")

↪ *"In many respects, stress is the wear and tear your body endures."* (A reality that Jeff Davidson and others have aptly reported.)

TIME TO FOCUS
Seven "Friends" of Negative Stress

↪ **Distress**   ↪ **Tension**

↪ **Fear**   ↪ **Anxiety**

↪ **Depression**   ↪ **Worry**

↪ **"Eustress"**

—Lloyd Elder

By any of these accounts, the harrowing effect we typically think of as stress is the way our body and mind warns us of pressure or perhaps danger to our well-being, real or imagined. It is also the way we try to prepare ourselves for whatever challenges that pressure brings: whether that is a fight for survival, performance of a task at some high level of intensity or endurance, or perhaps the means of escape. As you might have guessed, constant or prolonged preparation like that can have a nasty effect on your body, and your psyche!

Reflection: As you seek to take charge of your stress, what are your own thoughts, insights, and feelings about stress that you want to apply.

3. Impact of Physical Symptoms of Stress

One of the first places stress shows itself is in your body, and may even extend throughout your physical system. The reason stress is associated with physical "wear and tear" is because of the involuntary changes that occur in your body as a part of stress. Your body begins sending you signals and preparing itself for pressure as soon as your brain is convinced there's trouble ahead. (As noted in <u>Stress Management: A Comprehensive Guide to Wellness,</u> p. 149, by Drs. Charlesworth and Nathan, abstracted by Lloyd Elder)

- Digestion slows so blood may be directed to the muscles and brain.

- Faster breathing for oxygen.

- Heart speeds up.

- Perspiration increases.

- Muscles tense, may quiver.

- Chemicals release to clot blood more rapidly.

- Sugars and fats pour into the blood to provide fuel.

While these physical responses do often aid us in confronting a stressor in the short-term, sometimes they are actually counter-productive: when the energy we need is for concentration and not activity, or when the response far outpaces the need. Ultimately, continuous stressors put a tremendous amount of strain on the body—calling up all of those resources: the muscles, the hormones, the heart activity, will eventually exhaust the system if stress is not managed properly. A rubber band though flexible breaks when pulled too tightly.

Personal Reflection: When I am under stress in an interpersonal experience, my voice invariably moves to a higher range—probably registering emotional and physical response. What are your most noticeable physical responses to stress?

4. Study Resource: The Physical Nature of Stress

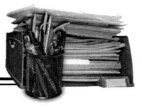

A Study Abstract prepared by Lloyd Elder:
STUDY RESOURCE: THE PHYSICAL NATURE OF STRESS
From: Reaching Out: Interpersonal Effectiveness and Self-Actualization
by David W. Johnson (6th ed.), Boston: Allyn & Bacon, 1997; pp. 289-296.

Dr. David Johnson asserts that "humans, as a species, are stress-seeking." Stress has long been linked to human problems such as headaches, ulcers, and muscle pains. But boredom (low stress) can make us just as sick as high stress. He goes on to explain concisely the physical responses to "the nature of stress" (p. 290).

"Another important aspect of stress is that the human body reacts to stress in a stereotyped, physiological way. Briefly, the autonomic nervous system and the endocrine system combine to speed up cardiovascular functions and slow down gastrointestinal functions. This equips us to take physical action to restore the situation and our internal physiological state to normal. It really does not matter whether we are reacting with great joy, or great fear, our physiological response is the same. To understand stress sully, homeostatis must first be understood. Homeostasis is the ability to stay the same. The internal environment of our bodies (our temperature, pulse rate, blood pressure, and so forth) must stay fairly constant, despite changes in the external environment, or else we will become sick and may even die. Stress alerts our bodies that action is needed to adapt to the external environment by changing our internal environment. The body then strives to restore homeostatis. Stress, therefore, can be defined as a nonspecific, general response of the body, signaling a need to perform adaptive functions so homeostatis can be restored."

Reflection: In high stress situations, how does this describe your body responses?

5. Emotional Responses to Stress: Healthy and Harmful

What we are more familiar with, and can usually spot in ourselves and others, are the emotional responses to stress. As church leaders, counseling others who are experiencing emotional distress is often a central function of our duties. But how often do we neglect our own emotional stress in the process? It is either because we don't believe "we" should be having such trouble or because we have not equipped ourselves for that kind of self-knowledge and attention.

"From the ends of the earth I call to you, I call as my heart grows faint; lead me to the rock that is higher than I." —Psalms 61:2

One of the central contentions of this study is that to have the strength and resources to effectively lead, counsel, and mentor others in the church, we need to develop the skills it takes to manage our own stress—physically and emotionally. The following topic explores the various emotional manifestations of stress—but treated in a self-assessment format.

A cartoon quip: ***"I feel much better, now that I have given up all hope."*** Now put yourself in the picture! Various studies have discovered a wide range of emotional responses to stress—some of them mild, others quite severe; some quite positive and desirable, and others negative and harmful. Not all responses are common to each person or at each experience of stress. Consider your own emotional responses to stress during the last six weeks or so as you read through the following list of possibilities.

Stress Tantrum Mat

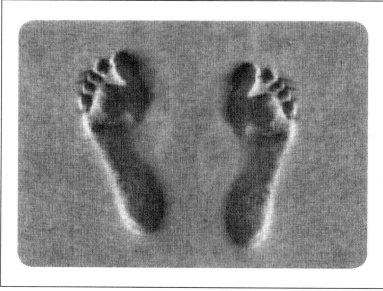

DIRECTION:

✤ *Place both feet on the mat.*

✤ *Jump rapidly up and down.*

✤ *Screaming is also permissible.*

✤ *If symptoms persist, call your doctor.*

Going to the mat is not recommended, so keep in mind not all emotional responses to stress are negative. Nevertheless, most of these are associated with some level of stress.

6. 20 Emotional Responses to Stress: Self-Assessment Form

Developed by Lloyd Elder from Scripture and Other Sources:

20 EMOTIONAL RESPONSES TO STRESS: SELF-ASSESSMENT FORM

Place a number beside each "stress response" that reflects your tendency to experience that feeling: 1—never; 2—seldom; 3—occasionally; 4—often; pay attention to the troubling ones:

EMOTIONAL RESPONSES TO STRESS   **Self-Assessment**

❖ **Anger/wrath**—a strong feeling of displeasure and belligerence aroused by real or supposed wrong; most often worsens stress experience, although there are times to be angry.   _____

  ↝ Proverbs 15:1—*A gentle answer turns away wrath, but a harsh word stirs up anger.*

  ↝ James 1:19—*My dear brothers, take note of this: Everyone should be quick to listen, slow to speak and slow to become angry.*

❖ **Anxiety**—Distress or uneasiness of mind caused by fear or misfortune; "a silent invader," the result of tension—that worried, troubled, uptight feeling that something bad or unpleasant is going to happen even if there is no real threat. This concept describes specific healthy and harmful emotional responses to stress.   _____

  ↝ Proverbs 12:25—*An anxious heart weighs a man down, but a kind word cheers him up.*

  ↝ 1 Peter 5:7—*Cast all your anxiety on him because he cares for you.*

❖ **Compassion/mercy**—a feeling of deep sympathy and sorrow for someone struck by misfortune; often accompanied by a desire to alleviate the suffering.   _____

  ↝ Proverbs 12:25—*An anxious heart weighs a man down, but a kind word cheers him up.*

  ↝ Colossians 3:12—*Therefore, as God's chosen people, holy and dearly loved, clothe yourselves with compassion, kindness, humility, gentleness and patience.*

❖ **Dejection**—disheartened; low-spirited; depression in spirit.   _____

❖ **Depression**—a common mood disturbance, a condition of general emotional dejection—even withdrawal—greater and more prolonged than warranted by any objective reason; a low state of functional activity; heavy-heartedness; melancholy blues.   _____

❖ **Determination**—the act of coming to a decision or of resolving something; a fixed intention to face a challenge.   _____

EMOTIONAL RESPONSES TO STRESS   Self-Assessment

❖ **Disgust**—a strong distaste, offensive to moral sense, loathing, strong aversion.   _____

❖ **Distress**—The dark side of stress; acute anxiety, pain, or sorrow; troubled, physical or emotional anguish that disables proper response to a situation.   _____

  ↪ Ps. 18:6—*In my distress I called to the Lord; I cried to my God for help. From his temple he heard my voice; my cry came before him, into his ears.*

❖ **Dread**—to fear greatly, to be reluctant to do, meet, or experience; to have fear or great reluctance.   _____

❖ **Eustress**—This is good news: (1) stress that is positive, an optimal amount of stress to respond to a particular situation; or, (2) stressors normally thought to be pleasant and desirable: new job, promotion, personal achievement, vacation, Christmas, marriage, birth of a child, etc.   _____

❖ **Excitement**—an excited state or condition; to experience awakened, aroused, or stirred emotions or feelings; stimulated to action.   _____

❖ **Fear**—alarm, dread, a distressing emotion aroused by impending danger, evil, pain—whether the threat is real or imagined.   _____

  ↪ Isa. 41:10—*So do not fear, for I am with you; do not be dismayed, for I am your God. I will strengthen you and help you; I will uphold you with my righteous right hand.*

  ↪ 1 Jn. 4:18—*There is no fear in love. But perfect love drives out fear, because fear has to do with punishment. The one who fears is not made perfect in love.*

❖ **Guilt**—a feeling of responsibility or remorse for some offense or wrong, whether real or imagined.   _____

  ↪ Hebrews 10:22—*...let us draw near to God with a sincere heart in full assurance of faith, having our hearts sprinkled to cleanse us from a guilty conscience and having our bodies washed with pure water.*

❖ **Happiness**—a quality or state of being happy, good fortune, pleasure, contentment; joy.   _____

  ↪ Jas. 5:13—*Is any one of you in trouble? He should pray. Is anyone happy? Let him sing songs of praise.*

EMOTIONAL RESPONSES TO STRESS   Self-Assessment

❖ **Jealousy**—resentfulness or enviousness, as of another's success, achievements, advantages; inclined to resentment or suspicions. _____

   ↪ *Gal. 5:19-20—The acts of the sinful nature are obvious …idolatry and witchcraft; hatred, discord, jealousy, fits of rage, selfish ambition, dissensions, factions…*

   ↪ *2 Cor. 11:2—I am jealous for you with a godly jealousy. I promised you to one husband, to Christ, so that I might present you as a pure virgin to him.*

❖ **Joy**—a feeling or state of great delight or gladness, as caused by something exceptionally good or satisfying; keen pleasure. _____

   ↪ *Ps. 4:7—You have filled my heart with greater joy than when their grain and new wine abound.*

   ↪ *2 John. 4—I have no greater joy than to hear that my children are walking in the truth.*

❖ **Pride**—self-respect, self-esteem; a feeling of gratification aroused from association with something good or laudable. _____

   ↪ *Ps. 16:18—Pride goes before destruction, a haughty spirit before a fall.*

❖ **Sadness**—a state of being afflicted by grief or unhappiness, of being sorrowful or mournful. _____

❖ **Tension**—mental or emotional strain; intense, suppressed suspense, anxiety, or excitement; could be positive or negative. _____

❖ **Worry**—feeling of uneasiness or anxiousness; to torment oneself with or suffer from disturbing thoughts; to fret, to be disturbed, to lose peace of mind, to be bothered, or tormented. _____

   ↪ *Mt. 6:25-27—Therefore I tell you, do not worry about your life, what you will eat or drink; or about your body, what you will wear. Is not life more important than food, and the body more important than clothes? Look at the birds of the air; they do not sow or reap or store away in barns, and yet your heavenly Father feeds them. Are you not much more valuable than they? Who of you by worrying can add a single hour to his life?*

7. Behavioral Response: Steps to Burnout

There is perhaps no greater internal threat to the life and leadership of a church leader than that of "burnout." The long hours, the dependence of so many others on your work, the kingdom-level stakes that the ministry takes on, coupled with the preponderance of financial strain, makes church leadership the same as all other "helping" and "non-profit" professions: highly susceptible to burnout.

Burnout is not the same as stress! Burnout is what happens when stress runs amok, the result of a series of behavioral and attitude changes that gradually build after the physical and emotional layers of stress have begun to take their toll under a lack of management. If disease is the ultimate physical threat of stress, burnout is the ultimate psychological threat.

Elements of burnout specific to ministry are dealt with in later chapters, with strategies for dealing with and avoiding burnout. But below read the basic behavioral steps that can accompany the road to burnout. Have you experienced any of these on a regular basis? You likely are studying this book because you are already concerned about stress and its effects. So think seriously and honestly about how far down the road to burnout you might already be, and prepare to take action as you work through the rest of this training program!

Three Stages of Stress: Remember, physical and emotional responses to stress are in large part preparation to fight and protect. Prolonged exposure to that level of demand has the same effect as running your car long and hard day after day. Eventually the machine gives out. Characteristic behavioral/psychological traits associated with each stage of the road to burnout are described by G.S. Everly in <u>Occupational Stress Management</u> (p. 186). Notice that from stage #1 to #2 to #3 is noticeably developmental, so there is value in acknowledging early when stress is moving toward burnout.

> Stage 1: Stress Arousal
>
> Stage 2: Energy Conservation
>
> Stage 3: Exhaustion/burnout

Reflection: It's really up to you as an individual to take charge of and act upon basic understandings. Spend a few minutes to review your understandings about stress and reflect on responses to the question: "What do I need to know; and what will I do about it?"

A Review Abstract prepared by Lloyd Elder:

STUDY RESOURCE: STRESS WARNING SIGNALS

A review abstract by Lloyd Elder

The Wellness Book: The Comprehensive Guide to Maintaining Health and Treating Stress-Related Illness, from Part 4, pp. 175-285, edited by Herbert Benson, M.D. and Eileen M. Stuart, R.N., M.S. A Fireside Book published by Simon & Schuster; New York, 1992

This book, resulting from 25 years of scientific research and clinical practice at the Harvard Medical School, seeks to combine the best of what you can do to enhance your health and well-being with the marvels of modern scientific health care.

Part 4, "Stress Management" (pp. 175-285), is composed of six chapters: 10. Managing Stress; 11. How Thoughts Affect Health; 12. Feelings, Moods, and Attitudes; 13. Coping and Problem-Solving; 14. Communicating; and 15. Jest 'n' Joy.

Stress is part of our lives; any change is stressful because change requires us to make adaptations. What causes stress in one person can be an exciting challenge for another. This resource admits to using "stress" in the common usage as "distress"—the negative cycle of chronic or excessive stress that reduces coping and performance. However, "stress-hardiness" emphasizes the positive characteristics of stress such as control, challenge, and commitment. One psychiatrist advocates the "five L's of success," of health and happiness: Learn, Labor, Love, Laugh, Let go.

The negative stress cycle can be avoided in the first place, but is difficult to interrupt: Stress accumulates … activates the "fight or flight" response … causes stress symptoms either physical (e.g. muscle tension, pain) and/or psychological (e.g. anxiety, worry) … in turn increases stress. Stress warning signals may differ from one person to another, but some are common.

STRESS WARNING SIGNALS *(continued from p. 182 of* <u>The Wellness Book</u>*)*

Physical Symptoms			
Headaches	Stomachaches	Indigestion	Right neck, shoulders
Back pain	Racing heart	Sweaty palms	Restlessness
Tiredness	Sleep difficulties	Dizziness	Ringing in ears

Behaviorial Symptoms			
Excess smoking	Compulsive eating	Grinding of teeth at night	Compulsive gum chewing
Bossiness	Overuse of alcohol	Attitude critical of others	Inability to get things done

Emotional Symptoms		
Crying	Unhappiness for no reason	Overwhelming sense of pressure
Easily upset	Edginess/ready to explode	Boredom/no meaning to things
Loneliness	Nervousness, anxiety	Feeling powerless to change things

Cognitive Symptoms			
Forgetfulness	Trouble thinking clearly	Inability to make decisions	Thoughts of running away
Constant worry	Memory loss	Lack of creativity	Loss of sense of humor

CHAPTER 10
Examining Common Causes of Stress

Stress and Life Experiences: Keeping Your Focus

A "stressor" is any phenomenon that triggers a stress response. Just as everyone's response is different, with some general tendencies for us all, every person has different stressors in their life and work. This chapter will introduce you to some general realms of common stressors. What is stressful to one person may not be to you, and what is stressful to you at a particular time may not be at another.

And, although you likely can list quickly the three or four known stressors in your own life, keep in mind that it is the hidden stressor, the one you're not prepared for or wary of, that may cause you the most damage. It's nearly impossible to "manage" stress that you don't see coming, or know is there! So keep an open mind to new ways of understanding possible stressors in your life and in the lives of those around you. That includes good stress, known as "èustress"!

In your life experience, stress has four or more levels of experience.

- **External stressors:** such as weather, social environment, family members, ministry associates, job expectations; holiday seasons; these all seek to penetrate your sense of well-being.

- **Internal stressors:** inside your life experiences—such as self-image, self-expectation, personality type, emotional and mental energy, level of physical health, etc.

- **Coping skills:** awareness, acceptance, coping responses, positive action, reasonable avoidance, Christian faith resources, etc.

- **Stress experience:** those stressors that make it all the way into your emotional/mental/physical center and threaten your sense of well-being.

> *"No matter how old you are, you always think that there may be something hiding under the bed."*—Monica, age 13 Youth Calendar

Common Stressor #1: Personality

That's right, personality. Sometimes the stressor component itself is not an outside entity but is a function of who you are (an internal stressor)! Tests have shown that a significant factor in stress is one's own personality. There is no key personality to a stress-free life, but by becoming aware of certain personality tendencies in your own life and ministry, you may be able to manage the danger points more successfully.

Type A personalities: The "Type A" personality is known for intense ambition and aggression toward meeting goals. If you find yourself exhibiting the following traits, you may be a type A person:

- highly competitive nature, often leading to flashes of temper and hostility

- intense obsession with achievement and urgency

- extreme "multi-tasking"

- obsessive perfectionism

- defending against criticism

Numerous studies show that the Type A person is more likely to experience heart disease due to chronically inflated blood pressure and other physical characteristics of

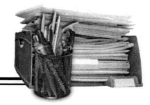

extreme responses to a variety of situations which would not become stressors in non-type-A individuals.

Self-Image: Seemingly on the other end of the spectrum, though not directly related, is the issue of self-image. Are you:

- often shy and self-conscious around others?

- quick to blame yourself?

- uncomfortable around superiors, peers, or members of the opposite sex?

Persons with extremely low self-image levels—in confidence, sense of self-worth and helplessness—can also lead to an increase in life stressors and a propensity for disease, most particularly cancer. Surprising studies have indicated that traits of a low self-image can both lead to the onset of cancer in individuals, and can limit one's ability to fight the disease once it appears.

Of course, there could be many explanations that make that relationship more indirect than direct, but either way, fighting against a low self-image may be essential to avoiding or at least putting off the ravages of cancer. As such, it turns out that the chronic response to "flight" can be as dangerous as a chronic response to "fight."

- **Paul's Self-Portrait:** The positive and negative sides of the apostle's inner personal life are sometimes revealed: 1 Cor. 9:25-27—*"Everyone who competes in the games goes into strict training. They do it to get a crown that will not last; but we do it to get a crown that will last forever. Therefore I do not run like a man running aimlessly; I do not fight like a man beating the air. No, I beat my body and make it my slave so that after I have preached to others, I myself will not be disqualified for the prize."*

- **Jesus taught his disciples:** *"I tell you the truth, unless you change and become like little children, you will never enter the kingdom of heaven. Therefore, whoever humbles himself like this child is the greatest in the kingdom of heaven."* —Mt. 18:3-4

Reflection: How would you define your own personality in your life and leadership? Do you often exhibit the traits of a Type A personality, or have a chronically low self-image?

Common Stressor #2: Change

Even if you are unaware of it being there, a stress response of some kind accompanies most every **significant change in life, work, and circumstance.** Adjusting and adapting to new realities is one of the most fundamental and common of all stressors. You don't have to feel fret, worry, or exhibit an active "stressing out" for these events to wear on your physical and mental equilibrium in a potentially damaging way.

This balance the body and mind naturally strive for is called "homeostasis," and the lengths we go to internally in order to achieve it in the face of change can often wreak havoc on important physical and mental activities. Even if the change is undeniably positive, this process takes place, and when it is extreme, can have negative consequences by forcing stress responses.

Moving, getting married, having a child, getting a new job all can be great events and can also cause stress responses in the healthiest of people. Of course, negative changes tend to have more damaging, and more prolonged, stress effects.

What are the most profound changes that have occurred in your life—for better or for worse—during the last two years? Did you know that the more you have had, the more susceptible you are to stress-related illnesses and difficulty, as a result of your resources for adapting being challenged? When change causes conflict, conflict may back into stressful experiences.

Reflection: As you monitor your own life and work, and in your capacity to lead and counsel others, keep in mind the impact change can have as a life stressor!

I eagerly expect and hope that I will in no way be ashamed, but will have sufficient courage so that now as always Christ will be exalted in my body, whether by life or by death.—Philippians 1:20

Common Stressor #3: Expectations

Two brands of "expectation" can easily become stressors: your expectation of yourself, and your own expectation of others.

- **Of You:** Everyone knows the feeling of pressure that can arise as a result of high expectation to perform in one's life and work. Often, the pressure we put on ourselves is even greater than what we feel from others. When managed correctly, this pressure can lead to great achievement and a sense of accomplishment and effort. But when mismanaged, or overburdened, the fear of failed expectation, or letting down yourself and others, can trigger stress responses that diminish performance levels in whatever you're trying to accomplish: lack of concentration, loss of sleep or appetite, and other stress responses can make any already-difficult task even tougher.

  This begins a debilitating cycle, as the sense of failed expectations easily translates to low self-image—you don't want your stress compounding like an annual interest rate! Proper management of expectation—not lowering expectations but managing them—is a key function of staying healthy enough to maintain effective leadership in the church or anywhere else!

- **Of Others:** Today's leadership demands require delegation and team-building and a reliance on others. This is healthy and a strong Christian leadership principle. It can also lead to disappointment in others when they fail to come through. Particularly in the church, we are often too quick to allow disappointment in the ethical lapses, or various failures in judgment of others to affect our own leadership capacity. Failed expectation from others can be a huge and complex stressor for a leader:

  - ✤ "If she can't do it, can it be done?"

  - ✤ "Was I right to place that responsibility in his hands?"

  - ✤ "You just can't trust people in this church/organization."

❖ Losing faith in team/family members/structure can have a highly negative stress impact on anyone. Turning that situation into a positive growth opportunity is not only a great challenge, but a necessary leadership trait in the church today.

Reflection: What, or who, is the greatest expectation stressor in your life?

"When your mother is mad and asks you, 'Do I look stupid?' it's best not to answer her." —Meghan, age 13 Youth Calendar

Common Stressor #4: Family and Personal

GLOSSARY: "RESPONSIBILITY"
from Princeton University's *WordNet*
The social force that binds you to your obligations and the courses of action demanded by that force.

Why is family a possible, even likely stressor in your personal life? Joy as it is, family is also a responsibility, one that does not go away with time, or can be left when the going gets tough like a bad job! Family stress can be caused by any number of very real and profound, personal responsibilities: health, illness, injury, death.

↗ **Financial responsibilities—** contributing to the welfare and well-being of the entire family unit. Money offers more stress-related obstacles than almost anything else. As a single person, you may seem to make financial decisions mostly for yourself; while sometimes stressful, that is

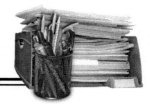

still an accountability ratio of 1:1. In a family, decisions and the decision-making process over making money, spending money, and saving money involves spouses, children, and sometimes parents as well.

- **Rearing children (even grandchildren)**—the awesome task of being a parent. Stress can come from all of the worry, desire, disappointment, and excitement you have for your children (and all of that usually comes in one day!). It is the greatest social responsibility we have, and can also feel like the most difficult. We not only have a responsibility to care for our kids, we also have to impart our sense of responsibility and values onto them as well, whether they like it or not! As you likely don't need to be told, opportunities for mismanaged stress here lurk everywhere!

- **Relationships**—Family is not just obligation, of course, it's also love and relationship—in fact that usually started it all! Maintaining and growing relationships with a spouse, with parents, siblings and in-laws can be a stressor for the same reasons as any interpersonal relationship: you can be dealing with issues of conflict, decision-making, communication, and trust.

Reflection: This is a good time to record your own thoughts about stress within your family.

Common Stressor #5: Vision and Purpose

Of the Future: Worry over the future can be an immense stressor. Whether grounded in a valid basis for concern, or a general anxiety about the future, this stress is real and can cause problems. Areas where vision of the future can cause stress:

- decision-making anxiety

- fear of failure

- worry that present success can't or won't continue

- general anxiety over the future

- fear of future medical problems/complications/relapses

- fear of future financial problems—debt/stock market decline/loss of income/ retirement

Vision of the future can be a stressor anytime we feel ill-equipped to deal with what's to come—whether it's certain or uncertain, positive or negative.

Of the Past: Reflection of the past can be a stressor when guilt, remorse, shame or loss lingers in our rear-view mirrors. Chronic stress over the past can lead to serious depression and can have serious negative impact on our physical and emotional health. Common past hauntings that can become stressors include:

- loss of job

- loss of loved one

- end of relationship/marriage

- regretted decision of any kind—interpersonal, vocational, financial

- wrong done to another

- physical/emotional traumatic experience

When the past is our own laboratory for learning lessons and self-understanding and improvement, it can be a positive arena of thought. But when we dwell on negatives from the past, like feeding a monster, negative stress responses are sure to come. Don't underestimate the impact your MIND can have on your BODY!

Reflection: Make a short list of your own future/past stressors.

Common Stressor #6: Frustrations

Lifestyle in the 21st century is a major cause for stress for every person. Modern-age stressors are technology, information, speed, speed, speed! For better or for worse, we have become accustomed to today's fast-paced society. The most wasteful stress responses, and unfortunately the most common, we experience today are really a result of modern-day advances. Why experience frustration over things generally not in our control? Things like:

- waiting in line

- sitting in traffic

- on hold—busy signal

- our crashing, confusing computers!

- service at stores, restaurants

Any time our immediate desires are delayed—or we perceive them to be—frustration can become a stressor that leads to anger and even, at worst, rage. This damaging stressor is really a function of our ability to accomplish so many things today in such a short period of time; so, frustration cycles can be not just daily but hourly phenomena if we fail to manage them.

Reflection: How much frustration does your stress response system take?

> *"Life is hard no matter how old you are."*
> —Rosalinda, age 13 Youth Calendar

Common Stressor #7: Life Overload

Anxiety and stress are not limited to individual challenges, events or circumstances. Sometimes perfectly manageable tasks or obligations can become stressful just by being compounded on top of one another! Something as simple as answering a phone call—routinely accomplished with no stress—can turn into a negative stressor when six calls are received in five minutes, or three people are on hold. Overload is one of the premier stressors in overachievers; those leaders with a clear grasp on their limitations are sometimes more able to keep down the number of balls in the air at once.

College students who insist on cramming their schedules with more credit hours than is recommended, parents who have to work overtime or more than one job to make ends meet, those in occupations that require wearing many hats at once, all are prime targets of the negative stress responses associated with overload.

The common danger is not that the responsibilities are by themselves more than the person can handle; it is the requirement to be constantly "on"—at work, or at home.

Daniel Girdano's thorough work, <u>Controlling Stress and Tension</u>, picks up on this theme of stimulation by defining overload as: "a level of stimulation or demand that exceeds the capacity to process or comply with that input; over stimulation" (p. 80). That text goes on to describe the overload effects of one of the most stressful known occupations—air-traffic controllers (ATCs):

> ATCs are faced with a combination of excessive time pressures, life-and-death responsibility, often insufficient support (either managerial or technical), and a virtually damning expectation for perfection from themselves and others. Research on these workers clearly demonstrates the stressful outcome of task overload…. Research has revealed that ATCs are occupationally predisposed to certain stress-related diseases, the most significant of which is hypertension, followed by peptic ulcers, and finally diabetes. The most highly stressful jobs of ATCs must certainly help explain why 32.5 percent of those examined in one study suffered from either gastric or duodenal ulcers (Girdano, p. 81).

Most of us are rarely required to perform such intensive tasks, requiring such constant focused attention, with such high stakes, as an air-traffic controller. But the message and pattern are clear. The constant rain of stimulation will eventually put you under water up to your neck, and beyond. And the overload danger of the minister should be taken very seriously: monitor the workings of the church; visit and comfort every ailing or troubled member; maintain a 24-hour, 7-day on-call status; attend his own family/relationship needs; and in the case of the bivocational or small church minister, take on another job.

Reflection: Do you try—or are you required—to do too many things at once or in rapid succession without a break?

Now that we have summarized seven different important stressors, it's time for honest self-evaluation and action. Each of the seven stressors, along with "other" is listed below. Add your personal thoughts and experiences. Which elements of your life or leadership do you identify as your biggest stressors in each category? Which might be causing significant stress responses in you that you hadn't noticed or given much attention? Will you be looking for management clues?

⤳ Personality:_____

_____

⤳ Change:_____

_____

⤳ Expectation:_____

_____

⤳ Family:_____

_____

⤳ Vision of the Future/Past:_____

_____

⤳ Frustration:_____

_____

⤳ Overload:_____

_____

⤳ Other:_____

_____

Study Resource: "How Stress-Resistant Are You?"

In addition to the seven common stressors set out above, quite often it is a pattern or cluster of seemingly small stuff that breaks down your resistance to stress. This study resource stands in support of the skills for identifying what makes you vulnerable to stress, but also with insight presents an approach to build up your resistance to stress. Use this as an assessment form but also as a strong ally for action planning to take charge of your personal or ministry stress.

TAKING CHARGE of Your *Time & Stress*

STUDY RESOURCE: HOW STRESS-RESISTENT ARE YOU?

quoted from *The Wellness Center Newsletter*, Belmont University, Fall 1995

Self-assessment questionnaires enable us to examine our current lifestyle, and then objectively measure behaviors and attitudes against established norms.

Instructions: Treating a score of "**1**" as something that is almost always true and "**5**" as something that is virtually never true about your stress reactions, circle the appropriate response for each of the following questions:

1.	I eat at least one hot, balanced meal a day.	1	2	3	4	5
2.	I get 7 to 8 hours of sleep at least 4 nights a week.	1	2	3	4	5
3.	I give and receive affection regularly.	1	2	3	4	5
4.	I have at least one relative within 50 miles of home on whom I can rely.	1	2	3	4	5
5.	I exercise vigorously at least twice weekly.	1	2	3	4	5
6.	I limit myself to less than half a pack of cigarettes a day.	1	2	3	4	5
7.	I take fewer than five alcoholic drinks a week.	1	2	3	4	5
8.	I am the appropriate weight for my height and build.	1	2	3	4	5
9.	My income covers my basic expenses.	1	2	3	4	5
10.	I get strength from my religious beliefs.	1	2	3	4	5
11.	I regularly attend social activities.	1	2	3	4	5
12.	I have a network of close friends and acquaintances.	1	2	3	4	5
13.	I have one or more friends to confide in about personal matters.	1	2	3	4	5
14.	I am in good health (including my eyesight, hearing, teeth).	1	2	3	4	5
15.	I am able to speak openly about my feelings when angry or worried.	1	2	3	4	5
16.	I discuss domestic problems—chores and money, for example—with the members of my household.	1	2	3	4	5
17.	I have fun at least once a week.	1	2	3	4	5
18.	I can organize my time effectively.	1	2	3	4	5
19.	I drink fewer than three cups of a caffeinated beverage per day.	1	2	3	4	5
20.	I take some quiet time for myself during the day.	1	2	3	4	5

Scoring: Add up all the points you have circled.

Interpretation: 20-45 You probably have excellent resistance to stress.

46-55 You are somewhat vulnerable to stress.

56-100 You are seriously vulnerable to stress.

Source: Test developed by psychologists Lyle H. Miller and Alma Dell Smith. Reproduced in C.L. Mee Jr., et.al. *Managing Stress from Morning to Night* (Alexandria, VA; Time-Life books, 1987) p. 27.

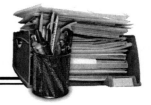

Study Abstract: "Stress Management—a Preventionist Approach"

You and I may not believe as does Richard E. Ecker that stress is a myth. But his thesis also includes a conclusion: "Neither life experiences nor relationships with others are ever the stressor. They may be the source, but never the stressor. It is our perception of the experience, event or the other person and our response that becomes the stressor."

STRESS MANAGEMENT—A PREVENTIONIST APPROACH
From *The Stress Myth* by Richard E. Ecker, University Press, Downers Grove, IL, 1985 – A review abstract prepared by Curtis B. Freed, MSN, LPC, Director of Counseling, First Baptist Church, Nashville, TN

In The Stress Myth, Dr. Ecker identifies a different approach to stress management. Based on research, conducting workshops and case studies the author describes a "preventionist" approach as opposed to the "interventionist" approach so popular for the last four decades. Look for the Ecker twelve laws and the biblical basis which undergird his "preventionist" approach to stress.

❖ **Thesis**: Stress is a myth. This myth is based on the belief that stress is inevitable and "exists primarily because the true meaning of stress has become lost in an abundance of alternative definitions."

❖ **Definition**: Stress is not a happening, an experience or force in the external world. It is a physical response that the human body invokes in order to deal with a perceived threat to stability. Stress is an adaptive response to an individual interpretation of an experience or relationship.

❖ **Purpose**: The author's purpose is twofold: 1) to develop insights and understanding to confront unwanted stress, 2) to show how God's power can help us engage the preventive approach to stress.

❖ **Stability**: Every individual develops a set of beliefs about our world and a set of values and guiding principles that provide emotional stability when subjected to uncertainty.

❖ **Premises**:

1. Whenever the stress response is appropriate to the body's physical needs, there is no excess stress and no stress exhaustion.

2. Stress prevention eliminates the need for stress intervention.

3. That "every individual can, through faith, commitment and practice, learn to react to life in ways that do not provoke excess stress."

4. Fundamentally, stress-motivated behavior is a plan for control and power. Control over the individual is seen as the cause of stress.

- ❖ Neither life experiences nor relationships with others are ever the stressor. They may be the source, but never the stressor. It is our perception of the experience, event or the other person and our response that becomes the stressor.

- ❖ If we understand where the stress comes from, we will experience two benefits:

  1. We will improve our ability to deal constructively with other people.

  2. We will be able to assess our own stress reactions and take steps toward stress prevention.

- ❖ The author differs with the interventionists – those who advise us to learn relaxation techniques or prescribe some medication to help us deal with stress. Ecker proposes a preventionist approach.

- ❖ **Prevention:** The creative alternative to so-called inevitable stress. Prevention eliminates the need for intervention. It frees us from unwanted stress.

- ❖ **Ecker's Laws:** The author gives twelve laws that provide the construct for his preventionist approach. Several are given here:

  - If the stress response is greater than the need, the perception is always wrong.
  - Excess stress promotes excess stress.
  - It is impossible to control the events of life.
  - Stress will not alter the outcome.

- ❖ Four rules to implement the preventionist approach:

  1. Understand what stress is.

  2. Accept the responsibility for your own stress.

  3. Find out the real identity of the source.

  4. Get in touch with your own identity. A person's self-image is a product of his other belief system. For the Christian, self-image has its roots in God's Word and in creation.

- ❖ Seek ye first the kingdom of God and all these things…

Study Abstract: "Humor in Stress Management"

Before Dr. Gary Flegal gets to the place of humor in taking charge of your stress, he underscores basic understandings of stress. But he puts a fine point to lessons about "humor" as a source of power in health with the experiences of stress.

A Review Abstract prepared by Lloyd Elder:

STUDY RESOURCE: HUMOR IN STRESS MANAGEMENT

from Stress Management: Practical Technique for You developed and edited by
Gary L. Flegal, Ph.D. (A.B.D.), Baptist Mind/Body Medical Institute, Nashville, TN

What is Stress?

Stress is simply the body's response to change. Everyone undergoes stress to some degree on a daily basis, but few of us know how to deal with it effectively. Most of us try to avoid stress instead of realizing it can be a positive element in our daily lives if we develop the skills necessary to manage it constructively. Because stress occurs daily and cannot be completely avoided, coping with it is a key to being healthy.

"Fight or Flight"

The biological response triggered by stress is called the "Fight or Flight Response." It includes:

- ❖ Increased blood pressure
- ❖ Increased heart rate
- ❖ Increased rate of breathing
- ❖ Increased blood flow to the muscles
- ❖ Decreased blood flow to stomach
- ❖ Increased metabolism

The common denominator between these physical changes is that they prepare you for physical action. This involuntary response is a survival mechanism preparing us to meet a physical challenge (fight) or to escape from danger (to flee).

Illness is Stress-Related

If your body experiences these fight or flight responses frequently or for long periods of time, illnesses such as heart attacks, ulcers or intestinal problems can develop. Doctors believe that up to 75% of an illness is stress-related. Therefore, to reduce these long-term effects of unresolved stress, it is important to learn ways to handle stress effectively.

Stress—Neither Good nor Bad

Stress is not negative. Stress is neutral. It is neither good nor bad. It is your response to a stressor (the thing that causes stress) that determines whether or not stress will be positive or negative for you.

Same Feelings—Different Interpretations

The physical responses (increased blood pressure, increased heart rate, etc.) are the same for both positive and negative stress. It is our interpretation of the situation as to whether we label the stress as "excitement," "challenge," or "fear" and "anxiety." We even have a different language for the two. If a stressor is labeled positive you might say that you have "butterflies in your stomach." If the situation is negative for you, your response might be that it "wrenches your gut." Same feeling—different interpretation.

HUMOR & HEALTH—THERE IS A CONNECTION

Sources of Power

Laughter and humor are potential sources of power, creativity, and health in our personal and professional lives. While not offered as a cure-all for every problem that exists, humor has a lot of positive possibilities for our daily lives:

1. Humor makes life fun.

2. Humor can help us cope with problems.

3. Humor with a hint of playfulness is a safety valve for aggression and an acceptable means to express anger.

4. Humor offers perspective and balance.

5. Humor is a means of communication and creative expression.

6. Humor provides temporary relief from society's restrictive regulations.

7. Humor is a way to express the truth even when truth is feared and repressed.

8. Humor is mentally and physically good for you.

9. Laughter affirms life and brings people together.

10. Humor often succeeds where other methods have failed.

Getting Started

Learning to use more humor requires practice. Here are some guidelines to help you get started.

1. Look for humor throughout your day; brighten your room or workspace.

2. Start a humor first-aid kit. Stock it with things that are funny to you—cartoons, jokes, greeting cards, a bottle of soap bubbles, comedy tapes, etc.

3. Make time for fun. Schedule a 10-minute humor break every day.

4. Share laughter with those around you.

5. Laugh when you are low. Psychologist William James said, "We don't laugh because we are happy—we're happy because we laugh."

CHAPTER 11
Identifying Seven Stress Factors in Ministry

Stress in the Vocation of Ministry:

Every vocation offers its own unique challenges and stressors. Certainly, work in the ministry is no exception. In fact, like most occupations stress in ministry has the capacity to energize high performance and achievements. It also tends to get out of control easily if not properly managed. And all recent indications are that ministers are not finding themselves able to manage properly the stressors of the job and life. Look at these alarming statistics, taken from a 1991 survey of clergy by the Fuller Institute of Church Growth:

- 75% reported a serious stress-related crisis at least once in their ministry.

- 50% felt unable to meet the demands of the job.

- 92% felt inadequately trained to cope with job demands.

- 90% work more than 50 hours a week.

- 53% averaged 5-6 hours of sleep per night.

- 85% spend 2 or less evenings per week at home with their families.

- 40% don't take a regular day off.

- 70% had a lower self-image than when they started in ministry.

- 40% had a serious conflict with a parishioner once a month.

- 50% had considered leaving the ministry within the preceding three months.

- 73% had no one they considered a close friend outside of marriage.

- 33% consider ministry hazardous to their families.

- 81% of clergy feel their families have been negatively impacted by the church.

Reflection: As in many other business vocations, how many of these stress categories fit your ministry experience as well? Many of these stress factors respond to specific training; others may respond to planned team response. Critical Stressors at Business:

- Job loss

- Job transfer

- Workload

- Competition

- Supervision

- Travel

- Meeting budget

- Office conditions

- Technology

- Boredom

- Your listing?

This chapter will explore many of the stressors and stress issues that seem particular to those in ministry. There will be an activity at the end that will allow you to respond to each stress factor with a thoughtful, personal evaluation of your susceptibility level, similar to the activity in the previous chapter.

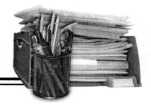

Factor in Ministry #1: Role Model Stressors

> **KEY TEXTS**
>
> *John 13:15—"I have set you an example that you should do as I have done for you."*
>
> *Mt. 6:24—"No one can serve two masters. Either he will hate the one and love the other, or he will be devoted to the one and despise the other. You cannot serve both God and Money."*
>
> *1 Cor. 11:1—"Follow my example, as I follow the example of Christ."*
>
> *1 Pet. 5:3—" ...not lording it over those entrusted to you, but being examples to the flock."*

A church is an institution whose mission revolves around a moral life, ethical relationships, and a commitment to follow the path of Christ. This can subject a minister or lay leader to very high standards: in personal life, and in relationships with staff and congregation. High standards, or the perception of them, can easily become the preeminent stressor in the life and work of a church leader, paving the way to countless personal and organizational problems if mismanaged. In the rush not to disappoint those who have entrusted you with this status, the true inner self of a minister can quickly become lost, while constantly juggling the needs and images others have of church leadership.

If you have ever found yourself:

- assuming a "pastoral persona" only when relating with congregation members;

- overhauling practices to appease the one critic in a sea of compliments and praise;

- needing to be serious most all the time in your official role; then you may be placing yourself under extraordinary stressors, even if you don't feel it... yet.

How/Why Do Churches Cause Stress?

- ✤ Absence of, or no sense of a church vision
- ✤ Church is not growing, and who is at fault
- ✤ Conflict in the congregation over whatever
- ✤ Opposes major values, programs, and ministries
- ✤ Resistance to changes of any kind
- ✤ Relationship skills

- ✤ Internal staff or member problems
- ✤ Church budget problems, real or feared
- ✤ Diversity of worship styles
- ✤ "Just don't like the preacher"
- ✤ Leadership style
- ✤ Preaching style
- ✤ Pastoral duties
- ✤ Professional development

It is often believed that ministers, as "Holy Persons" of the church, have achieved a connection with God that is greater, more authentic, or more important than that of any other person in the church or community. Often, this can even become the minister's own self-perception. When accepted, these expectation levels and assumptions will undoubtedly lead to feelings of failure and inadequacy. When handled improperly, high expectations will become a debilitating stressor, rather than the opportunity we hope it will be—not because of what is being done to the church leader from the critics outside, but because of what the self-image stressor does on the inside. You will know the role-model stressor is taking its toll when striving to be a Godly person and leader begins to feel like a burden. You feel the people in the church and community placing this burden on you, and even more heavily, you feel it from yourself! The responsibility to be open, accountable, ethical, moral, and holy is greater in the ministry than in any other vocation; and perhaps rightly so!

Reflection: This first responsibility of a church leader can also become the first healthy step toward taking charge of your unhealthy stress.

Factor in Ministry #2: Financial Stressors

Financial stressors of one kind or another are a fact of life in virtually every leadership occupation. As a minister, you take on additional financial burdens. Two major elements of financial stress dominate the life and work of the church leader:

- **Limited resources**: Churches depend on weekly tithes for operations, ministries, and salaries. It is too common for incoming monies to experience under-budget periods; tithes can become unpredictable with congregation turnover, economic conditions, and seasonal impacts, while the costs of running the church often stay constant. Most churches—particularly small and new churches—cannot afford significant reserve funds for times of calamity or a downturn in contributions. As an ongoing concern, finances can be (it almost goes without saying) an enormous stressor for a minister, who is often responsible for shepherding through the budget process, and appealing to members for contributions in times of crisis. No pastor wants to give a quarterly message on tithing, yet tight budgets and the stresses that follow could become the rule rather than the exception in church finances.

- **"Conflicts" of interest**: As a minister, your salary is determined by, and paid by the members of the church you serve. You have a financial responsibility to yourself and your family, and you also regularly preach the virtue of sacrifice and the danger of riches. As a servant of God's Kingdom, and of your congregation, you may often feel internal pressures associated with salary and responsibility—to serve God, to serve your congregation, to serve your family, and maintain yourself.

Reflection: Finances, personal and congregational, are often among the top three stressors. How about you?

> *Be shepherds of God's flock that is under your care, serving as overseers—*
> *not because you must, but because you are willing, as God wants you to be;*
> *not greedy for money, but eager to serve;…—*1 Pet. 5:2

But seek first his kingdom and his righteousness, and all these things will be given to you as well.—Mt. 6:33

Factor in Ministry #3: Kingdom Mission Stressors

From some perspectives, the role of minister is of greater impact than "life-and-death." Your mission concerns the very soul of your congregation and community, and it comes as a calling from God. The stakes of duty could, in this respect, not be higher. The stress of doing the work of God, and stamping that occupation right on your nameplate or business card, can be daunting if not managed properly. The pressure to grow the church, to minister to your congregants' spiritual needs, and to fulfill the will of God—in the very place where the will of God is the primary topic of discussion and prayer—can be hazardous to your physical and emotional health, especially if you take each offering and each invitation as a personal referendum.

By the same token, a church staff is often entirely made up of individuals who feel a similar calling, and similar occupational responsibility to the will of God. Working with a ministry team with this same strong sense of kingdom duty can be truly elevating when there is agreement and things are going well; it can also be a source of great conflict and stress when there is disagreement among those who feel strongly as to God's will. This stress of conflict can emerge within the church staff, within a church body, within a denomination, and all with potentially devastating results on the institution and the leaders within it. To be sure, no cultural realm has produced more stress and conflict in the history of the world than that couched in religious, theological, or spiritual disagreement!

> *"I will do the best I can with what I have, where I am, for as long as I can for Jesus' sake today."*—from John Wesley

> *"Carry each other's burdens, and in this way you will fulfill the law of Christ.... for each one should carry his own load."*—Gal. 6:2, 5

Factor in Ministry #4: Counseling Stressors

Church ministers have the responsibility to speak not only on a congregational level, from the pulpit, but also on a more personal level in counseling sessions with members. He

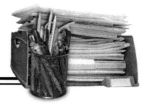

or she must lead with the organizational whole of the church in mind, but must also lead for the sake of the individual well-being of each congregant. Looked at this way, it's quite an awesome responsibility! Rarely do ministers feel completely comfortable and competent in both the institutional and the interpersonal roles.

The stress of counseling, or stress transferal, can be caused by any number of important factors:

- A sense of unpreparedness to properly advise or comfort the very real, and often very substantial, problems introduced in a counseling session.

- The time required in giving real, honest, sincere listening and counseling to every church member who asks for it.

- The emotional toll that can be taken when investing oneself in the life-problems of another.

- Helping a troubled person overcome adversity might be very spiritually uplifting, but trying to give earnest attention and help to the perpetually anguished, or those with serious and ongoing emotional, family, financial, or spiritual concerns can begin to detract from ministry to the church as a whole, involvement with one's own family, etc.

Reflection: Take stock of the counseling factor in your stress level.

Factor in Ministry #5: Family Stressors

Families of ministers experience stress in at least two primary ways:

- **The Fishbowl!** If you think it's bad for you, imagine what it's like for your family! Not only are you expected to be the holiest person in the church, yours is expected to be the holiest family as well! Families of church leaders commonly feel

the stress of fishbowl living, in which every problem seems to be known and magnified throughout the congregation. Spouses and children are often held to similarly high expectation levels with regard to ethics and decorum. And, also similarly, families can often perceive this pressure even when it is not there, or is minimal.

⌐ **No Time for Family!** While preaching the virtues of family values on Sunday morning, the on-call schedule-demands of ministers often leaves them little family time of their own. The big events in the life of nearly every congregant can become a responsibility for the church pastor: weddings, deaths, births, illness, loss of job, spiritual needs. Ministering and attending to the needs of all the families in the church can make the church leader's own family feel less important, or will leave the family in a poor state of communication.

> *"But if a widow has children or grandchildren, these should learn first of all to put their religion into practice by caring for their own family and so repaying their parents and grandparents, for this is pleasing to God."* —1 Tim. 5:4

> *"From now on there will be five in one family divided against each other, three against two and two against three."* —Lk. 12:52

> *"As long as it is day, we must do the work of him who sent me. Night is coming, when no one can work."* —Jn. 9:4

Reflection: Do members of your family need to create "crisis" to get your attention? You can see the damaging spiral that responses to this stressor might create for you and the people you love the most.

Factor in Ministry #6: Job Performance Stressors

Setting aside the high expectations, the Godly calling to do the work of the church, and the magnitude of the life-issues at stake, just doing the work from week to week can be a tough task! Being a minister requires:

- **Strict (and regular) Deadlines**: Your congregation is meeting on Sunday morning, Sunday evening, and Wednesday evening, whether you're ready or not! As a church leader, you are often required to be prepared to speak at all three events.

- **Long Hours:** From hospital visitation to committee meetings, sermon or Sunday school preparation to counseling sessions, performing a wedding on Saturday and participating in services on Sunday, the work of the minister or lay leader can be extremely demanding time-wise.

Who Me?

Too Many Hats

- **Versatility of Skills:** Church leaders are often required to be theologians, counselors, motivational speakers, business executives and worship planners all rolled into one. Every minister wants to be confident, competent, and effective in all the tasks of church leadership, and most enjoy and feel especially able in one or two important roles, but how many of us are truly in our element doing everything the job demands? Continued education in interpersonal skills, in business skills, in Scriptural knowledge, in communication skills and psychology are all a must.

- **Managing Triangulation:** See Study Resource, "Church Triangles Cause Ministry Stress."

> *"...his work will be shown for what it is, because the Day will bring it to light. It will be revealed with fire, and the fire will test the quality of each man's work."* —1 Cor. 3:13

> *"Drive thy business; let it not drive thee."* —Benjamin Franklin

Reflection: When the skills that are most lacking or least enjoyable begin to show through, and the stress response kicks in, what do you do? Identify stress factors that have been most acute in the last three months. Be specific and be looking for help. "What are you actually going to do about it?"

Factor # 7: Our Human Frailty Stressors

Throughout the naming of the several stressors above, there is at least one common thread: a minister of the gospel is subject to the same frailties as those "ordinary people" being served.

- **First, frailty does exist:** This is a truism often admitted to by folks on every hand, sometimes far too willingly. Ministers also quite readily accept this fact of human nature. We have to live with it and its force 24/7, without relief and with denial of very little.

- **Second, frailty causes stress:** Ministers are often faced with stressors from others caused by their frail nature, such as an unforgiving spirit, impossible

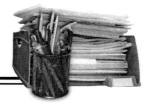

expectations, and unrealistic time constraints. On the other hand, ministers cause stress for themselves by suffering unwarranted self-doubt, saying "yes" to impossible tasks, and lacking a healthy dose of humility. What shall the minister do? Through years of experience, the best antidote I know of is to accept and practice the biblical message of sinfulness **and** redemption.

Reflection: Identify stress factors that have been most acute in the last three months. Be specific and be looking for help as you move forward in this book. Taking Charge means you deal with the question: "What am I actually going to do about stress factors in my ministry?"

- Work through the assessment opportunities found in this and other books on stress.

- Do a time-analysis of how you spend the hours of your ministry time as related to the total of 164 hours per week.

- Request a knowledgeable third-party to reflect with you about your stress experience and its impact on your life and ministry.

- When ministry skills that are most lacking, or least enjoyable, begin to show through as stress, what do you do?

TAKING CHARGE of Your *Time & Stress*

A Study Abstract prepared by Lloyd Elder:

STUDY ABSTRACT: "CHURCH TRIANGLES CAUSE MINISTRY STRESS"

from *Creating a Healthier Church: Family Systems Theory, Leadership, and Congregational Life*, Ronald W. Richardson, Minneapolis: Fortress Press, 1996

What is a human triangle, or "triangulation"? Briefly, it is when one person in a conflict with a second invites a third to enter the conflict and take responsibility for its resolution. Let's give this an actual ministry situation: Edward Education (A) has an ongoing conflict with Mildred Music (B) over the Wednesday night church schedule. Edward (A) seeks to get Pete Pastor (C) to take his side and become responsible for resolving the issue. A and B is a one-to-one (dyadic) relationship, which normally could and should manage the situation. C joins A to form a triangle of two against one B. In emotional systems, like families and churches, that increases anxiety (stress) for A and B and adds stress to C. C may also secretly side with B and confuse A completely. Resolution does not come easily, if at all (see Richardson, pp. 114-130).

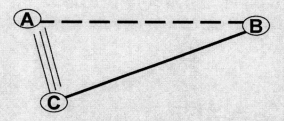

Triangulation causes anxiety rather than resolving it. Richardson (p. 129) gives some clues about responding, as follows:

1. Remember triangles are normal, but not necessarily helpful.

2. Be clear about your own role in the triangulation process.

3. Since triangles are about other people's anxiety, what could you do to contribute to a calmer, safer environment?

4. Become an able resource in the system by recognizing triangles and their driving emotions; be less reactive; stay in contact with the human elements, including your own; ask good questions.

5. Don't jump into every triangle that comes along.

Reflection: How often do you get tangled into triangulation?

A Study Resource Adapted by Lloyd Elder:

STUDY RESOURCE: "MAJOR EVENT ASSESSMENT CAUSING STRESS STRESS"

from "The Social Readjustment Rating Scale" by Thomas H. Holmes & Richard H. Rahe
published in *Journal of Psychosomatic Research*, 196

What The following test is based on the premise that good and bad events in our lives can increase stress levels and make us more susceptible to physical and mental health problems. It also weaves together personal and work events and situations. Directions—check the following major life/ work events which have taken place in your life in the past six months. Then calculate your stress level index by adding up the given points for each event or experience.

Major Events/Experiences

_____ 100 Death of a spouse

_____ 73 Divorce/separation

_____ 63 Death of close family member

_____ 53 Personal injury or illness

_____ 50 Marriage

_____ 47 Fired from work/ministry position

_____ 44 Change in family member's health

_____ 40 Trouble with the congregation

_____ 39 Employment change/retirement

_____ 38 Change in financial status

_____ 36 Change to a different line of work/ ministry

_____ 35 Change in number of marital arguments

Major Events/Experiences

_____ 32 Change in work responsibilities

_____ 29 Trouble with in-laws

_____ 28 Outstanding personal achievement

_____ 27 Change in church activity

_____ 25 Change in living conditions

_____ 24 Revision of personal habits

_____ 22 Change in work hours, conditions

_____ 21 Change in residence

_____ 18 Change in social activities

_____ 16 Change in sleeping habits

_____ 15 Change in eating habits

_____ 13 Vacation

_____ 12 Christmas season

_____ **Calculate Your Total Score and Use for Assessment**

Life Stress Assessment: This Life Stress Assessment shows some life pressures that you could be experiencing. Depending on your coping skills, this index may indicate the likelihood of stress-related illnesses. Potential stress-related illnesses could be mild such as frequent tension headaches, acid indigestion, or loss of sleep to very serious illnesses like ulcers, migraines, and cancer. After calculating your total score in the left-hand column, apply to the following stress levels. **0—99:** Low susceptibility to stress-related illness; about 10% likelihood of mild stress-related illnesses. Relaxation and stress management skills can help you cope with minor life stressors. **100—249:** Mild to moderate susceptibility to stress-related illness; about 30-50% likelihood of illness. Learn and practice relaxation, stress management skills, and a healthy, lifestyle. **300 and above:** Major susceptibility to stress-related illness; about 80% likelihood of mild to very serious stress-related illnesses. Daily practice of relaxation and stress management skills is very important for your wellness before a serious illness erupts or an affliction becomes worse; professional consultation may prove helpful.

TAKING CHARGE of Your *Time & Stress*

A Study Abstract Adapted by Lloyd Elder:

STUDY ABSTRACT: "ANALYSIS OF TIME FACTORS CAUSING STRESS"

from pp. 16-18 of Time Management for Ministers by Mark Short Nashville: Broadman Press, 1987

A survey conducted by the Baptist Sunday School Board reported in 1985 that seven of the top ten stress factors identified by ministers were related to time-particularly the lack of it. The other three stressors among the top ten related to expectations for productivity and leadership. Approximately the same amount of stress was reported by the various classifications of ministers, but the causes of stress were not the same. For pastors, the two items with the highest percentage of stress were too many demands on their time (21.5%) and inadequate retirement plans (18.8%). For ministers of education, the top two stressors were too many demands on their time (21.7%) and administrative responsibilities (10.5%). The two highest stressors for ministers of music and ministers of youth were too many interruptions and too many demands for their time. The top ten stressors for pastors were:

- too many demands on my time
- lack of study time (reading time)
- administrative responsibilities
- lack of time to visit prospects
- expected to take the lead in everything and to be a motivator
- too many interruptions
- demands for productivity
- groups in church expecting different things of minister
- too many promotional materials to read
- establishment of time with family.

Much has been written about stress that leads to burnout in ministry. These ten stressors point to that type of growing frustration. One of the better solutions for dealing with burnout is to draw support from the church leadership in an act of shared responsibility.

The minister's family is not exempt from time pressures. A 1983 survey (conducted by D. G. and Berlie McCoury and reported by Jim Hightower in "Proclaim") asked 250 pastors' wives to establish the major stressors in the parsonages. Eight stressors were clearly identified in this order: (1) time pressure, (2) the husband's needs and expectations, (3) financial pressures, (4) church pressures, (5) parenting pressures, (6) lack of friends and family needs (a tie), and (7) personal expectations. In this helpful editorial, four helpful suggestions were given to the pastor's family: be yourself, encourage your wife to be herself, schedule weekly time for your wife and your children, and expect love, care, and affirmation from your people and give it freely in return.

Both surveys point to the management of time for the minister and minister's family as a major problem in the church. Careful evaluation of the time-robbers might aid in corrective scheduling and, therefore, less stress to all involved.

Reflection: Where do you see yourself in the picture? Note your personal reflections, assessment, application, and action planning. Each ministry role is both common to all and unique of itself. Reflect on your unique ministry stressors.

CHAPTER 12
High-Stress as Burnout:
Patterns and Prevention

1. Discovering and Guarding Against Burnout

✤ **"Just what is "burnout in ministry?"** The objective is to establish practical ways to discover and to guard against excess stress in life and leadership. The term "burnout" actually comes from the process of a rocket engine flame going out, because its fuel—which is burned to create the rocket's firepower (literally)—has been used up, or shut off. Before getting to the good news, it may seem to get even worse. Understanding the burnout incurred by stress mismanagement will hopefully be a strong motivational tool to encourage you to manage your own stress effectively.

Burnout is the ultimate, downward spiraling result of ignored stress, like the condition of a car run for too long, too hard, and with no maintenance. It has also been suggested that *"high stress for a person is like running an auto engine at full throttle without the transmission in gear."*

TAKING CHARGE of Your *Time & Stress*

The Apostle Paul seemed always living on the edge. Although a faithful and productive servant of the kingdom cause of Christ, he seemed always on the verge of burnout in every respect; spiritually, emotionally, and physically. He communicated at the deepest level to the Corinthian church: ***"But we have this treasure in jars of clay to show that this all-surpassing power is from God and not from us. We are hard pressed on every side, but not crushed; perplexed, but not in despair; persecuted, but not abandoned; struck down, but not destroyed. We always carry around in our body the death of Jesus, so that the life of Jesus may also be revealed in our body."***—2 Cor. 4:7-10

✤ **What are three progressive burnout stages?** A helpful list of progressive burnout symptoms has been reported by George Everly, published in his article, "Occupational Stress Management." Such an analysis may assist a minister to identify the level of stress, and to pursue skills and practices that properly respond. Everly identifies these three major stages of burnout:

- **Stage 1: Stress Arousal**—includes many of the elements of stress experienced. These are physical and emotional stress responses that are experienced by all of us at times: anxiety, increased heart rate, irritability, lack of concentration, sleep deprivation, etc. If persistent and left unaddressed, these common stress responses may lead to Stage 2.

- **Stage 2: Energy Conservation—** your mind and body recognize the jeopardy you are in, so the instinct to hold back and conserve kicks in. This can include, according to Everly, procrastination, cynicism, lateness (for work or with work production), withdrawal from others, etc. And finally, when stress is so badly mismanaged, the fuel is shut off completely and burnout sets in.

- **Stage 3: Exhaustion—**resulting in inconsolable sadness or depression, persistent digestive problems, chronic physical and emotional fatigue, the desire to completely "drop out" from work, family, society in general, and in the worst instances, even thoughts of committing suicide.

Where does stress start?   Does it ever end?

❖ **Burnout in ministry as a helping professional:** Ministers often experience similar patterns to other helping professionals. Studies have shown that "helping professions" are the group of occupations most susceptible to professional burnout. Clearly, church and community ministry are right at the heart of the helping professions. Whose work engenders more "devotion to a cause" and expectation to "emergency response to needs of other persons" than the Christian minister? In addition, William Turner, (writing in "The Quarterly Review," January-March,

1985, p. 19), aptly applies this to the preaching ministry of a pastor, presenting the following symptoms of pulpit burnout:

- A lack of enthusiasm in delivery

- A lack of energy in preparation

- Repetition

- Voice level, incompatible with sermon content

- Preaching too long

- Borrowed crutches, using other's sermons, outlines, too many quotes, illustrations, humor, can all indicate burnout.

✤ **Six general categories of ministry burnout:** A picture of the minister in burnout can include a number of symptoms in addition to those of pulpit burnout described by William Turner. Six general categories, of varying levels of concern, are listed below:

- Chronic lack of motivation/onset of depression

- Recurring hostility or defensiveness over work in the church or church office.

- Excessive work and work time on mindless tasks, persistent avoidance/ procrastination of important work.

- Denial of one's call to ministry; serious consideration of change of profession; belief that one's church leadership may not in fact be the will of God.

- Chronic illness and fatigue, repeating extremes in sleep or appetite patterns.

- Aberrant behavior; inappropriate activity, perhaps in public; as a cry for help/ attention, a conscious or subconscious desire to be free from the ministry.

Reflection: Read and consider the above assessment of ministry burnout symptoms. Write a brief description of any thoughts that you have—whether you have seen in

others or felt in yourself any of these. Do any of these, or could any of these, sound like you or someone you know?

❖ **Burnout Danger Zone:** All of the factors of stress, and the occupational tendencies of church leadership, work together to make ministry a burnout "danger zone." Patterns of unrealistic feelings may arise if stress is not handled correctly:

　‑ Pastors tend to feel indispensable, with a congregation and staff totally dependent on the availability, and invincibility of its leader.

　‑ The minister's belief that the work of the Lord is greater than oneself seems to require and reward sacrifice and a loss of self in the process.

　‑ The "suffering" may seem always to outnumber the "comforted." If the calling of a minister includes to clothe the naked, feed the hungry, and heal/comfort the afflicted, that work may seem never done.

　‑ Faith that God will ultimately provide the strength may be misplaced, especially if you continue in the same flawed existing patterns of behavior.

All of these can help church leaders to the conclusion that resting, or whatever might be needed for refuel, is not an option. But this is not, and can never be, the case. Once the stress limitations, dangers, and opportunities are acknowledged, then the road to burnout recovery or prevention can better be pursued. Refueling can and must be done, even in the ministry! The fire that led you to the work of the church, and that confirmed your calling as you began, can be maintained and enhanced, and if lost, it can be regained!

Reflection: Read and consider the above assessment of ministry burnout symptoms. Write a brief description of any thoughts that you have—whether you have seen in others or felt in yourself. Do any of these, or could any of these, sound like you or someone you know? Move ahead—thinking, resting, and working!

TAKING CHARGE of Your *Time* & *Stress*

STUDY RESOURCE: "ANALYZING THREE STAGES OF BURNOUT"
from G. S. Everly, p. 186, Occupational stress management. In G. Everly and R. Feldman, eds., Occupational health promotion. New York: Wiley, 1985. Cited in Controlling Stress and Tension, 5th ed. by Daniel A. Girdano, George S. Everly, Jr. and Dorothy E. Dusek. Boston: Allyn and Bacon, 1997, '93, '90, 1986, p. 78

Note: These stages usually occur sequentially, from Stage 1 to Stage 3, although the process may be interfaced or can be stopped at any point.

Stage 1: *Stress Arousal (includes any two of the following symptoms)*

- Persistent irritability
- Persistent anxiety
- Periods of high blood pressure
- Bruxism (grinding your teeth at night)
- Insomnia
- Forgetfulness
- Heart palpitations
- Unusual heart rhythms (skipped beats)
- Inability to concentrate
- Headaches

Stage 2: *Energy Conservation (includes any two of the following)*

- Lateness for work
- Procrastination
- Needed three-day weekends
- Decreased sexual desire
- Persistent tiredness in the mornings
- Turning work in late
- Social withdrawal (from friends and/or family)
- Cynical attitudes
- Resentfulness
- Increased alcohol consumption
- Increased coffee, tea, or cola consumption
- Apathy

Stage 3: *Chronic Exhaustion (includes any two of the following)*

- Chronic sadness or depression
- Chronic stomach or bowel problems
- Chronic mental fatigue
- Chronic physical fatigue
- Chronic headaches
- The desire to "drop out" of society
- The desire to move away from friends, work, and perhaps even family
- Perhaps the desire to commit suicide

A Study Resource Adapted by Lloyd Elder:
STUDY RESOURCE: UNDERSTANDING STRESS AND BURNOUT
from Quest Travel Seminars, http://www.questtravelseminars.com

There are two types of instinctive stress responses that are important as part of our understanding stress. Although this is significant, they are not acceptable as a full response pattern for coping with stress. The two instinctive responses are:

- "Fight or Flight," as a short-term response to a stress experience
- "General Adaptation Syndrome," a long-term pattern of response to stress experiences

"Fight or Flight": Some of the early research on stress conducted by physiologist Walter Bradford Cannon established the existence of the 'Fight-or-Flight' response (1932). His work showed that when an organism perceives a threat or experiences a shock, it quickly releases hormones that help it to survive. These hormones help us to run faster and fight harder. They increase heart rate and blood pressure and deliver more oxygen and blood sugar to power important muscles…. In addition, these hormones focus our attention on the threat, to the exclusion of everything else. All of this significantly improves our ability to survive life-threatening events.

Unfortunately, this mobilization of the body for survival also has negative consequences…. In this state, we are excitable, anxious, jumpy, and irritable. This then reduces our ability to work effectively with other people. Since our body and mind is in this heightened state, it is then difficult to concentrate, make good decisions, or rationalize.

"General Adaptation Syndrome": Endocrinologist Hans Selye, 'Father of Stress,' looked at the long-term effects of exposure to stress and identified the 'General Adaptation Syndrome.' Selye identified that when pushed to extremes, organisms reacted in three stages:

- 1st — Alarm Phase: reaction to the stressor
- 2nd — Resistance Phase: resistance to the stressor
- 3rd — Exhaustion Phase: resistance is exhausted and resistance declines

In the business environment, these three phases are developmental, with the exhaustion phase contributing strongly to what is commonly referred to as 'burnout.'

Reflection: Information and strategies regarding "ministry burnout" seeks to provide encouragement and coping skills—where are you in the journey and what could you be doing? Note your personal reflections, assessment, and application to your ministry.

2. Managing Stress/Preventing Burnout

Hopefully, if you weren't convinced already, the previous pages have convinced you that unmanaged stress over a prolonged period of time is damaging to personal health, and healthy relationships to others. It also makes your work inefficient and ineffective. We like to think that great sacrifice is needed to achieve great things, but piling on burden after burden does not translate into mountains of accomplishment and contribution. What it does, is to make you unhappy and unproductive (in work, in ministry, in family). So why do it? Patterns of mismanaged stress can become habitual and routine. But these habits can and must be broken! Here are some steps for anyone to follow in managing high levels of stress.

- ✤ **Step One: Know and Love Yourself:** Already in this study, you have taken some of the important steps to know and understand your tendencies and stress points. Sometimes, being aware of and on the lookout for your own symptoms of stress response and the situations that cause it make up half of the battle of stress management! Here is another handful:

  - The Third Commandment: Jesus gave the second greatest commandment, that actually includes a third—***"And the second is like it: Love your neighbor <u>as yourself.</u>"*** (Matt. 22: 39) This Step One is for taking charge of high stress, but also for every other area of life.

  - Care enough about your ministry and yourself to want to maintain total health, spiritually, socially, mentally and physically. Do whatever it takes to reaffirm your self-esteem (counseling, prayer, meditation, study) and your pride as a participant in God's Kingdom, beloved by your Creator. Again, recall "The Serenity Prayer" by Reinhold Niebuhr:

    > ***"God grant me the serenity to accept the things I cannot change; courage to change the things I can; and wisdom to know the difference."***

  - Become cognizant of those personal danger areas you've identified and act accordingly. Sometimes the perspective of knowing what can give you

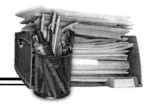

stress before you get there can neutralize its negative effects, especially "the little things."

- Many times a particular stressor is not worth the harm it is causing! Realizing that alone can reduce the level of stress involved. Did you know that quirk of your office-mate, or the morning traffic, or some other bothersome thing, was actually causing you to get "worked up"?

- Make a list of the little things that bother you, but aren't truly significant hindrances to your important tasks. Look it over, and then throw it away. Do the same in your own life with the little things. Toss them aside and get on with your day! You and your work and your family are too important to get sidetracked by many of the things we let get under our skin. Learn to laugh at those little things, rather than becoming miffed. Sweating "the small stuff" may be needless and fruitless stress.

- Know your limitations: If disappointment in yourself is one of your stressors, set goals and schedules—both short and long-term—that are reasonable and that acknowledge the "real you." You are not Superman or Wonder Woman. Remember the things that are in your control, and the things that are not. Of course, set high standards and be ambitious, but give yourself and your team a chance to succeed.

- Follow a schedule that organizes your time in a way that acknowledges your stressors. If there is a particular regular deadline that provides weekly anxiety, why not give it more time earlier in the week? Do you confront a recurring "difficult person" in your life or work? Devote the time that's due that person, and then move on. It's not just effective time management, it's having a conscious awareness that stress spreads like an infection from one area of your life to another. Decide that you will no longer let stressors run your life in a negative way.

Reflection: As you consider your own desire to know and love yourself, one survey has shown additional practices have been actively pursued to cope with stress:

TAKING CHARGE of Your *Time & Stress*

TIME TO FOCUS:
SURVEY OF COPING STRATEGIES

- *Direct Action—46%*
- *Acceptance—30%*
- *Distraction—27%*
- *Redefinition—25%*
- *Catharsis—25%*
- *Relaxation—17%*
- *Social support—15%*
- *Religious support—6%*

Psychology (Benjamin, p. 490)

❖ **Step Two: Take Care of Your Body:** As we said at the beginning of Part 2, stress is as much a physical response to conditions as it is a mental/emotional one. Regular exercise will keep your body prepared to handle negative stress when it happens. It also helps you work off the effects of ongoing stressors. Some standard-care activities are really very simple! Such as:

- **Breathing**—Zondervan's Complete Stress Management Workbook, pp. 229-30, describes a correct way to breathe healthily—about a dozen breaths per minute, expanding your lower rib cage, not lifting your chest. Incorrect breathing during every day life can compound other stress responses. The lack of oxygen coming in can leave you exhausted, with headaches and poor circulation.

- **Exercise**—Regular and reasonable exercise will improve your overall wellness; even just some extended walking and stretching. Do not overextend, of course, and set moderate goals. Try to do exercises you enjoy, and make it a regular part of your schedule, not an after-thought "when you have time."

- **Nutrition:** Take care of what you put into your body! Nutrition goes hand-in-hand with exercise in keeping you well. Antioxidants—found in fruits and vegetables, as well as fish, almonds, and other foods containing vitamins A and C, beta-carotene and other nutrients—help protect your body. Caffeine, sugar in high doses, excess salt, and smoking are all making your body's job harder.

Reflection: *"Carry each other's burdens, and in this way you will fulfill the law of Christ....for each one should carry his own load."* (Gal. 6: 2 and 5) *and "Each of you should look not only to your own interests, but also to the interests of others."* (Philippians 2:4)

- ❖ **Step Three: Be a Person, Not Just a Role or Function** (don't try to go it alone)

  - You are not defined solely by the roles you play in life! You are not just an employee holding down a ministry position. There it is now and raises the question: Do you have to wear so many hats that you lose track of the person that's underneath them? Parent, spouse, boss, carpool driver, cook, mediator, counselor … and the list goes on and on. Are you still in there somewhere?

  - Remember, you are a person who needs honest relationships of integrity. Disclosing your true feelings, enjoying a moment, pursuing a hobby, getting to really know those in your life and letting them really know you—these are all ways to stay in touch with your true self, underneath all of your external functions.

  - Of course, the **integration of** our true selves with our positional roles is a most valuable and significant experience. That is the most complete way to live and to serve. So don't let yourself get lost in all the hats you must wear, and make sure that you spend some time just being yourself, not actively performing a function of responsibility.

- ❖ **Step Four: Don't Be Afraid of Stress, Use it if you can.**

  - **Stress can be a good thing,** let it play on your team. Do not always lineup against stress as an opponent. Recent research into stress has begun to highlight all the ways in which stressors can actually be good for you, can propel you into the best performance, the most focused concentration, and the most successful outcomes of your life.

> *"Stress exposure is the most powerful stimulus for growth in life. People invariably grow the most in areas in which they've been pushed the most. Stress exposure expands stress capacity."*
> (**Stress for Success**, James Loehr, p. 4)

✍ **Opportunity for Challenge:** This view of stress emphasizes the opportunity for a challenge and the great rewards that can come from demands for high productivity in life and work. Overcoming the potentially negative effects of stressors by being prepared to turn that energy into positive output is the heart of stress management. And like high-level exercise, the more you work through your stressors in a positive way, the more stress you will be able to take on skillfully.

TIME TO FOCUS: MANAGING STRESS
- ✍ *Be realistic*
- ✍ *Limit change*
- ✍ *Talk it over*
- ✍ *Learn to relax*
- ✍ *Improve your environment*
- ✍ *Seek help*

(Scriptographic booklet on Managing Stress, p. 13)

✍ **Embracing Stress** is the insightful and well-supported stress message from Gary E. Parker, in <u>Creative Tensions: Personal Growth Through Stress</u>, p. 17:

> *Instead of trying to avoid tension or tranquilizing it, we will be better served if we embrace it, if we jump into it, if we accept it for what it is (or can be). Stress can serve us well as a teacher, as a sharpener, as a whittling knife for life, if we willingly see it as an ally in the maturing process. Stress can kill us, to be sure, but it can also birth us…. God's greatest servants were people who survived tough moments of stress. I wonder. Would Joseph have become the savior of his brothers and his nation if he had not suffered the stresses caused by the years of slavery and the allurement of Potiphar's wife? Would Moses have felt the kinship he did for his own people if he had not experienced the deadly fight with the Egyptian slave master? … Would Jesus have been able to so fully empathize with us in our struggles, if He had not endured the pressure of Gethsemane?*

❖ Step Five: Seek Guidance from Skilled Helpers

Through the years in my different ministry roles, I have found it helpful to seek out trained helpers. Stress has a way of closing windows of fresh air and pulling the curtains against the light of day. Seeking help has been regular, if not dramatic, and come about in several ways:

- Many times I have called into my confidence a wise specialist, explained the issues causing stress, responded to question, filled out my information base, discussed options, and proceeded with decision and action; quite often with more enthusiasm and greater success.

- Another source for a trained helper has come from among skilled colleagues. I have said: "Will you put on your other hat with me a bit? You know what is happening around here and how I am trying to respond. Talk to me from your experience about what I am missing and why this is causing me stress."

- As a pastor I was for many months in the same ministers support groups. Sure we talked shop, but we also talked ministry about this expectation, that program, the other staff members, etc. That informal mentoring often refreshed my outlook, made me feel less alone, or at times I was simply told what I ought to do. Although I am responsible for myself and my work, occasionally I actually did what I was told to do.

- Attending a selected workshop has turned into a targeted help just at the right time. I might leave the conference with my own set of notes and a list of possible actions. Stress is healthy if it drives you to pay attention to the help that is available.

- Sue and I have been professional helpers to many, and because of our family structure and needs, we have gained valuable help from others, some who are wise believers, experienced veterans, or trained specialists.

- Reading has often sent me to sit at the feet of people I have never met, only to walk away better able to take charge of my stress and to enjoy life, family, and work more abundantly.

Reflection: What are you already doing to reach out to your own set of professional helpers? And, perhaps what else could you do to take charge of your load of stress.

✤ Step Six: Let God Help and Guide You

Coping with our stress is not the primary reason for our relationship to God. Salvation is not essentially utilitarian—what we can get from God. Rather, we are redeemed to enjoy God and serve Him forever. Neither is our family bond to Him only to avoid hell and attain heaven. But for those inside the faith relation to a loving Father, **there is help** for every part of the earthly journey, including coping with stress, in ways such as:

- Allow gathered worship to cleanse and prepare your mind for each week. In worship we open our heart to a full array of life-changing experiences such as adoration, thanksgiving, redemption, instruction, and fellowship.

- Undergirding your life daily in personal worship should be preparation for each new day. Throughout time believers have claimed strength through prayer, Bible study, meditation, reflection, and resolution.

- Allow prayer to open your ears daily to God's message for you, and yours to God; the text in 1 Peter 5:7 encourages us, ***"Cast all your anxiety on him [God]** because he cares for you."*

- Allow your priorities as a Christian to keep you focused on your truest goals, and looking past those less important things that can become stressors if you let them.

CHAPTER 13
Ten Ways for Ministers to Manage Stress

Taking charge of your stress is not a new task to add to an already busy schedule! **Actually it is already part of your life-journey and ministry position description.** To develop and practice sound strategies to cope with ministry stress in a life-long healthy manner. The most pertinent question for each one of us to ask and answer is, *"What am I going to do about the stress in ministry that I encounter, and, also stress that I generate?"* Ministers have a unique set of stress challenges, but also unique outlets for managing the stresses that are peculiar to the work of church leadership.

Stress Relief Kit

INSTRUCTIONS:

1. *Make & clip target on wall.*
2. *Place hands on each side of target.*
3. *Then, bang head on circle until...*
   a. *Stress is relieved, or*
   b. *You are unconscious*
      (Not recommended)

BANG
HEAD
HERE!

TAKING CHARGE of Your *Time & Stress*

This chapter draws on research and experiences to collect and encourage proven skills and best practices for your life and work as a minister. You may be encouraged to find your strengths and stir up your awareness of ways to help manage the stresses of ministry, and even to turn them into positives for your life and leadership.

✤ **Faith: Practice what you preach.** The beginning and ending place to manage your stress in life and in ministry is to live out on a daily basis your own Christian faith. Let's put it into a personal commitment: *"I will try to manage stress by practicing what I preach."* A few "preaching points" may help apply this concept:

- **Love one another**: John. 13:34—*A new command I give you: Love one another. As I have loved you, so you must love one another.*

- **Daily life**: 2 Corinthians. 5:7—*We live by faith, not by sight.*

- **Example of Christ**: 1 John 2:6—*Whoever claims to live in him must walk as Jesus did.*

- **Fruit of the Spirit**: Galatians 5:22-23—*But the fruit of the Spirit is love, joy, peace, patience, kindness, goodness, faithfulness, gentleness, and self-control....*

- **Prayer**: Philippians 4:6—*Do not be anxious about anything, but in everything, by prayer and petition, with thanksgiving, present your requests to God.*

- **Follow His Word**: Ps. 119:105—*"Your word is a lamp to my feet and a light for my path."*

- **Positive Confidence**: Philippians 4:13—*I can do everything through him who gives me strength.*

- **Trust in the Lord**: Proverbs 3:5-6—*Trust in the Lord with all your heart and lean not on your own understanding; in all your ways acknowledge him, and he will make your paths straight.*

Reflection: A "Type A-Personality" person gladly quipped: *"I don't have stress; I give it."* You may even have humorously made this boast, but that really does not

represent the long-term profession you make with your life. More than that, we need to claim the promise and follow the instruction in 1Peter 5:7—*Cast all your anxiety [stress] on him because he cares for you.*

❖ **Approaches: Define your patterns of stress responses**. As a minister, and as a person, you may choose one of several approaches to managing, or mismanaging, your stress. Pick out the dominant approach you most often turn to, and assess how well you are doing. "Coping" may often be the most useful approach.

- **Denial**: *"I send stress underground; I don't acknowledge it even exists."* This may feel desirable, but stress will surface and be felt.

- **Avoidance**: *"I run the other way; my flight from stress manages me."*

- **Attacking**: *"I fight back; I hit stress head on, even if it worsens the situation and escalates the stress."*

- **Thriving**: *"I welcome stress, even invite it into my life. I perform best under high stress."*

- **Reducing**: *"I stay away from stressful situations, those I am not able to handle right now."*

- **Coping**: *"I face up to stress, usually with acknowledgment, reflection and with a range of proven skills."*

Reflection: For helpful treatment of "experience analysis," see pp. 129-132 of <u>A Manager's Guide to Self-Development</u> (3rd edition), Mike Pedler, John Burgoyne, and Tom Boydell; London: McGraw-Hill, 1994.

❖ **Analysis: Examine the stress situations.** As a minister, you face a continual flow of significant situations: ones that are challenging, difficult, or worrying. Why not use "situation analysis" to help cope with the stress involved? Here are some of the components of "stress analysis":

- Focus on a particular situation that needs stress analysis, one you have recently experienced or one coming at you right now.

- Identify the people involved, including you.

- Then try to recall your feelings, thoughts, actions, and behaviors—before, during, and after that stress situation.

- Reflect as carefully as possible on the experiences of persons in the room, such as Person #1 and Person #2: their feelings, thoughts, actions, and behavior. Though difficult, this is valuable in stress analysis to distinguish their similar and dissimilar reaction to an identical concept or event.

- To validate your judgment about the experience, check with the other persons involved. Did you misidentify their feelings, or incorrectly assume their thoughts?

- Do you understand one person better than another? Do you better assess their actual behavior than their feelings?

- Continue this "stress analysis" before, during, and after the event. Did your behavior authentically reflect your own stress level?

- **Benefits of analysis:** This approach can be adapted to match most situations in order to: improve your skill at self-understanding; focus on the true experience of others; deal with the substantial issues rather than creating new ones; understand the behavior and feelings of others; reduce stress or at least coping better; and bring a calmer, more responsive presence to such a significant experiences.

Reflection: Can you say, *"I understand myself and my stress-load pretty well; also I take a hard look at my strengths, limitation, values, and feelings."* And, "I am learning truly to understand others." By asking yourself questions, examine these five trustworthy skill-sets available in your practice of stress analysis and management:

- Prevention: "what stress can I manage by prevention skills?"

↩ Awareness: "what causes me stress now and as patterns?"

↩ Acceptance: "what causes me stress that I cannot change?"

↩ Coping: "what stress coping and practices do I depend on?"

↩ Action: "what stress can I change by specific actions and changed behavior?"

[For helpful treatment of "experience analysis," see pp. 129-132 of <u>A Manager's Guide to Self-Development</u> (3rd edition).

✤ **Structure: Set healthy boundaries.** Setting clear, healthy boundaries protects you and your interests in a relationship while still valuing the other person. Unhealthy relationships generate frustration and stress. By creating "rules" and within limits, you can eliminate unhealthy habits and stop letting others take advantage of you. Since a relationship is give-and-take, applying boundary rules consistently steers away from disruptive behavior and benefits positive behavior.

One of the surest ways to succumb to stressors is by organizing your day/time on the adrenaline rush of the "has-to-be-done." The life and work of the minister must have some structure that will keep the pressures of being on call "24/7" from overwhelming life. Remember, as a minister, you are no good to anyone if you are in the throes of emotional and physical burnout. The boundaries you set and live by will determine whether the stresses of ministry are managed effectively or not.

↩ **Time:** Do your meetings have ending points scheduled, as well as beginning points? Do you set aside time for long and medium-range thinking and planning? Do you plan for time alone and with your family, or do you and your family just get the left-overs? (See Part 1 of this book.)

↩ **Privacy:** This is one of the hardest issues for a minister to face: your work potentially involves meeting the needs of every part of a person's life. Crises can and often do arise at times other than "regular business hours." Do you have sufficient boundaries in mind, and in practice, that respect your and your family's privacy? Stresses begin to take over once you realize that you are not in control of any part of your life. Setting boundaries of privacy for yourself within reason is not abandoning your ministry. It's a way to give your ministry a chance to succeed.

- **Authority:** Are things set up in your church so that you are responsible for nearly everything? Work together with your church to set boundaries for responsibility and authority. **Delegate, delegate, delegate.** Trust others to handle important responsibilities and make clear everyone's role, so that you no longer have to be the filter for every inquiry and concern. This is no license to pass off responsibilities that are yours, but successful delegation will empower your volunteers and staff members, and will focus your leadership and streamline your church organization. Disorganization and lack of focus can be a key stressor in any leadership position.

- **Goals:** Do you sometimes feel as if your church is trying to do some of every imaginable thing? Are your efforts spread thin by ambition, honorable as it may be? When your goals are boundless, knowing how and where to start, much less how and where to stop, can be an enormous stressor. Work with your church and staff to set manageable goals of achievement and areas of involvement for your congregation's ministry.

- **Relationships:** In a copyrighted Internet article, Lisa Brock provides the following clues for setting relationship boundaries:

  - A successful relationship with boundaries (rules, limits) is one in which both parties benefit.

  - Each member helps the other in times of need, supports the other in the relationship.

  - When conflict arises, you work through it together toward a beneficial solution.

  - Answer the question, "Why do you let others take advantage of you?" "Because—
    - ◆ *I just feel so guilty.*

> ✦ *I need others to depend on me.*
>
> ✦ *It's really my fault.*
>
> ✦ *I don't deserve any better treatment.*
>
> ✦ *I seem to choose bad relationships."*

- Carefully consider and apply consistent and appropriate boundaries; it's worth the effort.

- Boundaries can be a way to increase the depth of friendship and respect with those who matter most.

Reflection: Can you say? *"I practice good interpersonal skills in relating to others.* How good are you at setting boundaries? Where should you start?

(See Article on http://www.troubledwith.com/—go to *"Stress, Troubled Times, Out of Bounds"* by Lisa Brock)

❖ **Attitude: Set your inner thermostat.** The church community should be a healthy, inviting place. Leading with a light heart and a gentle spirit can keep your stressors in check, as well as those around you. Some of these are excellent prevention skills:

- **Perspective:** Developing some perspective on problems may not help you solve them, but it does keep them from debilitating you. So, learn to laugh at yourself when you need to. Learn to focus your concentration on those things you can control, rather than fretting over those you can't. Learn to distinguish the big things from the small things ... and don't react the same way to both.

- **Humor:** Use humor in your sermons; tell jokes on yourself if it will help! Experts tell us every year that laughter is good for our health. It's good for your church's health as well!

- **Relaxation:** Use prayer, meditation and breathing techniques to keep you on an even keel, and not just when things are tough but every day. Being assertive is often useful in leadership, but being angry almost never is. Quick, crisp decisions can help keep your church moving and confident in your leadership, but rash frustrated decisions almost never do.

Reflection: Remember, stressors are not good or bad in themselves. How we manage them dictates whether stress will have a negative influence on our health and effectiveness as leaders. In short, stay in control of your own leadership attitude. It is one thing you know you can control, even if it seems nothing else is in your charge. And #1 among attitude priorities? "Be positive." It's contagious, and breeds success.

❖ **Community: Seek out supporting relationships.** Ministry work can be tremendously isolating if you allow it to be (many of you are nodding your heads, I can tell!). The demands on your time and your psyche, and the expectations of godly performance at all times will be magnified ten-fold as stressors if you retreat into social isolation. Building community both inside and outside of your congregation, folks with whom you can divulge all your concerns, is an essential element of warding off negative stress responses in yourself. Where can ministers go for this kind of rejuvenating community?

    Personal Confidant/Mentor: Sometimes a single relationship can be the most important combatant you have in managing stress. Is there a person in your life, a spouse, a best friend, a sibling to whom you can disclose your thoughts? Someone you can likewise listen to and trust? My minister/brother, Rev. Carl Elder, has been the most constant one for me. Talking to people who know you best is a powerful life force, a perspective on your place in life and leadership that extends beyond the horizon you yourself can often see. Strong relationships are one of God's greatest gifts to all of us. Ministers are no exception.

    Professional Confidant/Mentor: Is there a colleague in your association, a former teacher you trust, someone you have worked with in the past? Someone whose experience you trust? Talking with people who know your situation because they've been there before can provide professional perspective and help you learn from the mistakes or successes of others.

- **Ministry Team**: Your own ministry staff, the immediate community for your leadership challenges, should be a trusted group. This team can be the first line of defense in helping you and your church address potential stressors and manage them effectively. Do you try too hard to keep stressors locked behind your office door? With the exception of occasions when privacy concerns demand it, closing off your leadership team is rarely if ever a positive stress management strategy.

- **Ministers' Support Group**: Do you meet regularly with other ministers in your neighborhood or association? There is a good chance they are dealing with similar stressors you are! Even if no one has all the answers in your support group, it can be helpful, relieving and insightful, just to talk it over with others and know you are not the only one!

Reflection: Throughout the years of my ministry, I have always been in one or more of those invaluable helping groups. Of the 4 groups listed above, in which do you find the strongest, most helpful sense of community? Which should you spend more time cultivating? On the flipside, are you being a part of a helpful community for other ministers?

❖ **Assertiveness: Maintain healthy self-esteem.** Many of us have experienced the need to reduce stress by assertive behavior; so let's take a look at these suggestions:

- Build your own healthy self-esteem—value your thoughts, feelings, schedule, and goals.

- And, place a high value on the thoughts, feelings, rights, and expectations of others.

- Listen to others, really hear what they have to say and give honest, clear feedback.

- Take the risk of asking for what you want or is expected; don't be defensive, permissive, or judgmental.

⤳ Say "no" persistently and with respect; do it as soon as you know; but get right to work on your "yes."

⤳ Schedule your time with a sense of purpose, goals, direction, and outcomes.

⤳ Relax: plan some slack in your mental and physical activity.

⤳ Carry work or leisure material for inevitable "while you wait" periods.

⤳ Look for the humor, the joy, the surprise, the lesson in experiences.

⤳ Remember to love yourself and your family as you love others.

Assertive Management Overcomes Stress
(Key suggestions from Burley-Allen, Managing Assertively)
Assertive management or supervision may improve your skill in dealing with stress or anxiety. Consider the building blocks of managing assertively:
- building your self-esteem, a self-image
- knowing how to listen to others
- taking risks by asking for what you want
- giving constructive feedback--not permissive or judgmental
- saying "no" persistently and with respect
- handling criticism by being your own best critic
- giving and receiving positive feedback, praise, and strokes

(See Zuker, <u>The Assertive Manager</u>, pp. 162-183; and Burley-Allen, <u>Managing Assertively</u>. Also: See SkillTrack° <u>#7.4--Assertive Leadership</u>)

❖ **Family: Keep your family in central focus.** The family of the minister, whatever size or shape, is at the very core of the minister's life. It is both a resource for coping with stress, and also a source of stress. When your stress spills over into your family experiences, it sometimes escalates; so what can you do to provide "stress help"? Since you cannot, and should not, keep your own "stress" bottled up, your attitude and actions can help set the tone in stress reduction and coping within the relationship. How?

⤳ Cope with your own stress in the several ways and means we are considering here! Be a calm and attentive presence as a family member.

- Help to set reasonable boundaries between your family and your ministry; when needed, seek the congregation's help. Like the older family movie, "Cheaper by the Dozen," discuss items at the dinner table that are of "general interest."

- Be an understanding, caring minister to members of your family—but not the resident expert on all issues.

- Together set family goals, expectations, and values; don't be overly detailed.

- Work together as a family on selected mission/ministry tasks.

- Be intentional about family time and schedule. I had to learn this the hard way and return to this in every season of family life.

- Try occasional "stress analysis" since your family may be composed of various ages, shapes, schedules, knowledge, and interests.

- "Practice what you preach"; the family relationship is one of the most significant, and difficult, arenas to live as an authentic example.

- Honor the needs and values of each individual family member; healthy members contribute to a less stressful family.

- Be a calm presence in the midst of family life; don't let "blowing off steam" become your norm.

- Keep growing together in faith, in purpose, in self-understanding, and in family skills.

Reflection: On this aspect of the minister's life, Robert Dale has an excellent discussion in <u>Pastoral Leadership</u>, pp.213-224.

❖ **Presence: Overcome stage fright in public ministry functions.**

Your encouraging, confident presence is crucial in many areas of your ministry, and normal stress is often positive rather than negative. One of the most common experiences of stress is "stage fright"—a very real, often acute, kind of work-related stress: a nervousness, dread, or fear before and/or during a public performance before an audience. "Stage presence" is an appropriate response to overcoming "stage-fright." "Presence" refers to the fact of being present and also the bearing, behavior, and performance of a person. In this context, "presence" is the quality of self-assurance and effectiveness that permits the speaker/minister to achieve a rapport with the audience—eg. "stage presence."

Your ministry often requires preaching or teaching to your own congregation, making a presentation to a business conference, addressing a college chapel, or reading a paper at a professional meeting. Some nervous response can be normal, even energizing you to face the audience event. Severe nervousness, called "stage fright," creates a form of fight or flight response: dry mouth, sweaty hands, rapid heartbeat, upset stomach. What presence can you be and do to avoid or cope with such stage fright? We are going to summarize a set of proven practices:

- To begin with, prepare thoroughly; know what you want to say and how. Prepare an outline of major ideas and organize support material. Is your message born of faith and dependence on God?

- Review the speech, even rehearse it on location if possible; tape your voice for quality, and rate.

- Greet members of the audience as they arrive; demonstrating friendliness can build confidence.

- While you wait for the time to speak, practice stress reduction such as deep breathing; convert your nervous energy into enthusiasm.

- Use positive self-talk: that you are prepared; that what you have to say will help the audience; that they are on your side.

- Begin with a pause; don't rush; start with a sentence spoken from memory.

- Maintain eye contact and move naturally around the speaking area; use body language to express your message.

- Stay on message; avoid digressions or adding unplanned content.

- Focus some attention on selected visuals so that verbal delivery is augmented; don't dawdle over the obvious.

- Close your message with a summary (brief) of your main points, and warmly express appreciation to the audience.

- Expect your "stage experience" to be energized by normal stress rather than frozen by stage fright.

- (Helpful concepts have been included from <u>Business Communication</u>, 4th ed., by Mary Ellen Guffey. Mason, Ohio: Thomson South-Western, 2003, pp. 506-508.)

✤ **Mission: Live and Minister on purpose.** You are a messenger of God's love to those around you. He has called you to assist Him in the mission of extending His Kingdom on earth as it is in heaven! What greater cause could there be? What greater motivation? As great and unique as the stressors of ministry can be, there is an equally great and unique power and support available.

When stressors threaten to overwhelm you; when time is short, demands are high, and resources are low, remember your calling. Your purpose is noble, indeed heavenly! God does not ask you to do it alone, or to be more than the human you are. He needs you to be strong and healthy, in mind and in spirit. He needs you to be in a position, both internally, and as a part of a community, to do the best work you can do. This strength of purpose can be one of your greatest allies in managing stress. God has called for your service to others. When stress has taken a toll on your motivation, remember your calling and purpose. Will that one thought manage all your stressors for you? Of course not. But it should empower you to seek the strong tools you will need to answer God's call in the best way you can.

CHAPTER 14
Managing Ministry Stress:
Study Resources and
Abstracts

T he closing chapter seeks to make unique contributions to you as an interested reader, and to the completion of the study:

- If you are interested in additional and specific study in related areas of stress and stress management, these could serve you well. That is also one reason we have included an extensive, annotated Bibliography.

- The resources also enrich the contribution of the book because they provide special and expert opinion in areas that go beyond the text itself. Skilltrack® Leadership publications are cited as such also.

- These resources also provide fuller citations of material I used in my research and writing of the manuscript. A majority of the proven skills and best practices come from decades of ministry and noted authorities in the field of stress or ministry.

Study Abstract #1—Focusing on Stress Prevention Skills

Although stress prevention is presented by many terms throughout Part 2, this study resource is worthy of its inclusion to capture the insight of Warren Blank and to capsule what is meant by "proven skills and best practices." His premise is that successful leaders take a holistic approach to preparedness for their tasks, including the stress that goes with it.

A Study Abstract Adapted by Lloyd Elder:
ACHIEVING SUCCESS OVER STRESS
from <u>The 108 Skills of Natural Born Leaders</u> by Warren Blank New York: AMACOM, American Management Association, 2001, pp. 41-45

Author Warren Blank affirms that natural born leaders have stress, but the best leaders achieve success over stress. How? Most of the following skills and practices support the value of stress prevention. The stress of the work is there, but best leaders are prepared. His suggested actions include:

- Assess your level of physical and emotional stamina.

- Pay attention to physical activity and food diet.

- Audit your level of mental clarity and stability.

- Put worry in its place; expend your energy on analysis and action.

- Conduct a perspective audit: how important will this issue be five hours, months, or years from now?

- Consider your rest routine; the body and mind need balance.

- Review your lifestyle choices; include fun that keeps you alive.

- Review your work style mentality; expect excellence of yourself, but avoid perfectionism.

- Try "transcendental meditation" for a six-month period

Reflection: These methods require discipline, time, and action; but the benefits are worth it.

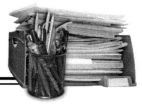

Study Abstract #2—Reducing Stress by Confronting Impending Stress

It is possible to accept and reduce stress by confronting stress ahead of time. Five steps are proposed which separate and face the stress level one at a time.

A Study Abstract Adapted by Lloyd Elder:
DESENSITIZING YOURSELF TO COMING STRESS
from <u>Asserting Yourself: A Practical Guide for Positive Change</u>
by Sharon Anthony Bower and Gordon H. Bower, pp. 53-57

"Desensitizing" is to your stress system like dipping your feet in hot water is to your pain threshold—entering a little bit at a time until the whole foot can handle the heat. It is future-oriented, aimed at reducing stress in a specific future situation: you picture yourself acting and reacting positively in successive events of increasing stress threat, leading up to the problem scene so that you will have less fear. When it actually hits you, the 5-step process recommended by Bower and Bower works like this:

1) Maintain deep relaxation as you imagine a frightening scene leading to anxiety or stress. "Tomorrow, I'm going to get fired."

2) Stay with the imagined scene with relaxation 10 to 20 seconds; mentally keep yourself in the picture.

3) Imagine the next scene in the progression of your discomfort: "I am going to work today for the last time." Stay with this image until your stress is reduced.

4) In a relaxed fashion, move to the next scene, still of lower threat, and face them with full mental effort and relaxation: "My appointment with Mr. X is in 15 minutes."

5) Complete the process with imagining the big one—the 100% stress threat level; inhale and exhale slowly and deeply and say, "Good morning, Mr. X. I have come to collect my last pay check and severance pay."

Reflection: Now choose a "stress threat" of your own and follow this process to imagine, pre-live, and desensitize yourself toward a more self-controlled, calmed presence. Of course, you may not need to use this in minor functional stress experiences; but in continuing, or in-depth stress, such reflective desensitizing may be most helpful. A calm presence for yourself is a goal of this process.

TAKING CHARGE of Your *Time & Stress*

Study Resource #3—Taking Charge of Stress through Time Management

Copied from SkillTrack® 12.1 Time Management by Lloyd Elder:
PRIORITY TIME MANAGEMENT
Nashville, TN: Moench Center for Church Leadership
"Time Management Matrix" by Stephen R. Covey in First Things First, p. 37

Reflection: How well do you manage your time? Poor time management contributes directly or indirectly to much of the stress in life and ministry. These four quadrants help you to diagnose your present time use, and indicate how you might make changes to reduce stress and enhance satisfaction. All four quadrants do have a place in your life. The goal is to invest more of your time in quadrant 4—Priority Ministry.

	Urgent	**Not Urgent**
Important	**3. Crisis Ministry** • Crises, deaths, funerals • Deadlines • Pressing problems • Many meetings, appointments • Hospital calls, counseling • Other: » **High Stress / Burnout**	**4. Priority Ministry** • Strategic thinking, planning • Problem prevention • Seizing opportunities • Sermon / teaching preparation • Relationship building • Evangelistic efforts • Professional development » **Productive / satisfaction**
Not Important	**2. Controlled Ministry** • Membership demands • Interruptions • Some mail, reports, phone calls • Scheduled meetings • Many popular activities • Brush fires » **Trapped / Driven**	**1. Trivial Pursuits** • Routine, busy work • Random mail, calls • Time-wasters • Many pleasant invitations • Procrastination activities • People distractions • Other: » **Boredom / Wasted**

Study Resource #4—Coping with Stress through Relationship Skills

GETTING ALONG WITH DIFFICULT PEOPLE

Summarized from SkillTrack® 7.5 <u>Resolving Conflict</u>, by Lloyd Elder,
Founding Director, Moench Center for Church Leadership, Nashville, TN

Remember, all of us are "difficult people at one time or another." In this book, as well as in life and ministry, taking charge of your time and stress are closely interrelated. Mismanaged time causes stress, and mismanaged stress often is a major time-waster. Let's summarize key elements of interpersonal conflict.

- ↩ Personal conflict is universal in human relationships; normal in patterns of behavior; and inevitable in most arenas of life, including Christian congregations. Conflict in its simplest expression is a situation in which two or more people desire and struggle over what is or appears to be mutually exclusive or incompatible.

- ↩ Whereas, church conflict within bounds may provide for vital fellowship, healthy spiritual growth, program improvements, and church expansion; out-of-bounds conflict often has a destructive impact.

- ↩ Troublesome church members most often function within negative, out-of-bounds conflict patterns. If permitted unlimited expression, such members can damage church leadership, unsettle the congregation, and diminish its ministry.

- ↩ Personality differences and conflicts are not only experienced today but were also in the New Testament era: among the disciples of Jesus over power and greatness (Mark 10:35-45), between Paul and Barnabas at Antioch (Acts 15:36-41), over the nature of the gospel at Jerusalem (Acts 15:1-21), between two women at Philippi (Phil. 4:1-3), and in a party spirit at Corinth (1 Cor. 1:10-17).

- ↩ An honest self-inventory of your own personal behavior patterns that contribute to conflict puts into practice the teaching of Christ: "Why do you look at the speck of sawdust in your brother's eye and pay no attention to the plank in your own?" (Matt. 7:3 NIV)

Reflection: These observations about interpersonal conflict set the stage for the one major source of stress. How can you improve and practice interpersonal skills in a way that reduces dysfunctional stress?

Study Abstract #5—"Hardiness and Resilience: Thriving on Stress"

Abstracts by Lloyd Elder from Two Sources

1st Resource:

THE HARDINESS FACTOR: SURVIVING THE STRESS OF CHANGE

Source—The Leadership Challenge, How to Get Extraordinary Things Done in Organizations by Kouzes and Posner; San Francisco, Jossey-Bass, 1987. (pp. 65-69)

❖ This research describes studies discovering the attitudinal distinction called "psychological hardiness." The authors found that, instead of associating high stress with illness, some stress can even energize us. Their personal best leaders were clear examples of difficult, stressful projects that generated enthusiasm and enjoyment.

❖ The big three, "commitment, control, and challenge," combine to block the strain of stress and its resulting illness. High stress/low illness executives were more committed to the various parts of their lives. They felt a greater control over things that happened in their lives; they experienced more positive challenge in change and development.

❖ Studies also revealed that family environment is the most important breeding ground for a hardy attitude. But organizations [including congregations] can do three things to develop hardiness among its leaders:

  ↝ to build commitment, offer more rewards than punishment;

  ↝ to build a sense of control, choose tasks that are challenging but within a person's skill level;

  ↝ to build an attitude a challenge, encourage people to see change as full of possibilities.

2nd Resource:

RESILIENCE: THRIVING ON STRESS

Adapted by Lloyd Elder from *Working with Emotional Intelligence* by
Daniel Goleman; New York: Bantam Books, 1998

✤ Daniel Goleman: "There are two kinds of stress—good and bad—and two distinct biological systems at work."

- Goleman describes "emotional intelligence" (sometimes called "EQ") as a new focus on personal qualities, such as "character and personality," initiative and empathy, adaptability and persuasiveness—most especially for leadership. He claims that IQ takes second position to emotional intelligence in determining outstanding job performance (pp. 3-5).

- He speaks of stress control by drawing a distinction between two executives of a regional telephone company filled with changing work stress. One executive is plagued by tension: "My life seems like a rat-race catching up and meeting deadlines—most not even important. So even though I'm nervous and tense, I'm also bored a lot of the time." The other executive thrives on stress: "I'm never bored. Even in doing things not interesting, I'm always out there straining to make a difference, to shape a productive work life for myself.

- The second executive was high in a quality called "hardiness," the ability to stay committed, feel in control, and be challenged rather than threatened by stress. This person bears the physical burden of stress much better, coming through with less illness.

- There is also a balance point when the sympathetic nervous system is pumping (but not too much), our mood is positive, and our ability to think and react is optimism. Here lies our peak performance." That is striving on stress! (see Goleman, pp. 88-89).

TAKING CHARGE of Your *Time* & *Stress*

Study Resource #6—"Practicing Servant Leadership: Serving with Stress"

1st Resource:
PRACTICING SERVANT LEADERSHIP: SERVING WITH STRESS
Copied from SkillTrack® 1.3, Servant Leadership Practices: Charting Your Course
by Lloyd Elder, Nashville, TN: Moench Center for Church Leadership

"Servant leadership in ministry is self-giving service with others after the pattern of Christ in order to achieve, by example and persuasion, extraordinary commitment and contributions toward mutually shared kingdom goals." **—Lloyd Elder**

- Servant leadership guards against stress and includes many of the skills and practices that equip you for taking charge of time and stress.

- Servant Leadership is explained in depth through three SkillTrack® CD-ROM courses: Principles (1.1), Pathways (1.2) and Practices (1.3).

- The more you understand the content and conduct of your leadership, the more stress may be channeled or dissipated.

- The more consistently you practice servant leadership the more you will welcome functional stress to help you achieve your purpose in ministry.

- The Graphic below shows five elements of servant leadership: 1) All five are interrelated in relation to one another. 2) Each has its own contribution to the practice of servant leadership. 3) They are seen in a 3-D format because the practice of servant leadership has a changing diversity of work to be done and of those to relate to.

- If the life focus of the minister is on the practice of servant leadership after the pattern of Christ, then pleasing Christ the Lord is the core of ministry, not merely the feeling level of relationships, events and happenings.

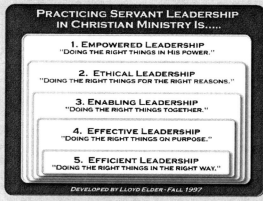

PRACTICING SERVANT LEADERSHIP
IN CHRISTIAN MINISTRY IS.....

1. EMPOWERED LEADERSHIP
"DOING THE RIGHT THINGS IN HIS POWER."

2. ETHICAL LEADERSHIP
"DOING THE RIGHT THINGS FOR THE RIGHT REASONS."

3. ENABLING LEADERSHIP
"DOING THE RIGHT THINGS TOGETHER."

4. EFFECTIVE LEADERSHIP
"DOING THE RIGHT THINGS ON PURPOSE."

5. EFFICIENT LEADERSHIP
"DOING THE RIGHT THINGS IN THE RIGHT WAY."

DEVELOPED BY LLOYD ELDER - FALL 1997

BOOK CONCLUSION
Your Journey of Ministry Leadership Development

"Taking Charge of Your Time and Stress" is a significant step on your journey of life-long ministry leadership development. It is our hope that this book is making a lasting contribution to the journey that you alone can choose for yourself.

Personal note: **My journey to the present has been related to the ministry of the church**. During my junior and senior year in high school, my first church position was as custodian of my home church. Then, in the summer of 1953, I was summer pastor of the Baptist Mission of Big Delta, Alaska, meeting in a log building. In several churches I was a student/part-time/bivocational pastor, then later in multi-staff congregations. For the past four decades I have been in ministry positions as administrator, executive, and educator. Through all these years, I have cared for congregational ministry. **That is why I'm still in ministry, and writing about it!**

"Taking charge of your time" is crucial because time is the very stuff of life. When you manage your time well—with purpose, balance, and priority—you are tending to the small bits and pieces of your life, and to the great epochs of your reason for being.

TAKING CHARGE of Your *Time & Stress*

"Taking charge of your stress" is not an effort to live a totally stress-free life, nor a binding work-driven life. Stress can be your friend. Managing your stressors successfully can turn them into positive, creative fuel for meeting your challenges and opportunities—for reaching the very heights in your life, leadership, and ministry.

The process of taking charge of your time and stress can be learned and put into daily practice. You can share it with others in your life. Taking charge—that is being responsible, faithful, and reliable—can motivate you, organize you, and connect you with your own best interest, disclosing your strengths and dreams to yourself. In short, you can bless your family with a more competent and encouraging presence, as well as develop into a more skilled leader and a more faithful servant in the kingdom of Christ. What steps will you take for your own sake?

Developing Ministry Leadership is a long-term, fervent goal for us. So, it seems appropriate for us to enhance the work of this publication with two concluding sections:

♦ *Time and Stress Bibliography/References/Annotations:* The last section in this book includes the full information expected on references cited or abstracted throughout the chapters. But beyond that, we have added resources and annotations of works and websites that support advanced research by ministers and students. Scan that for a sense of your own interest in works that we have reviewed for our study.

♦ *"Developing Leadership Skills and Practices:"* Continuing preparation for leadership in ministry includes, but goes far beyond "taking charge of your time and stress." As a closing study resource, a Skilltrack® Leadership article has been adapted for the longer journey of leadership development. The basis and process can be utilized with this book or any other resource as a roadmap for decisive, intentional ministry development.

A Study Resource by Lloyd Elder, Th.D. from SkillTrack® Leadership:

STUDY RESOURCE: "DEVELOPING LEADERSHIP SKILLS AND PRACTICES—THE WHY? AND THE HOW?"

in the ServantLeadersToday.com Library, "Experience Toward Leadership Excellence" (SL#1)

Humbling as it may be to read the statement one more time, I quote with agreement: "leadership can be learned, but it cannot be taught." That is yet another way of saying that leadership is like learning to swim or to ride a bicycle—others may help, but you have to learn leadership for yourself. The responsibility starts with the individual:

- From the Apostle Paul to Timothy: *"Do your best to present yourself to God as one approved, a workman who correctly handles the word of truth."* (2 Tim. 2:15 NIV)

- Stephen R. Covey—Seven Habits Revisited: *"And the endowment associated with Habit 7 renews the process of growth and development" (p.40). "Sharpen the Saw is the unique endowment of continuous improvement or self-renewal to overcome entropy; ... it is continuous improvement, innovation, and refinement" (p.47).* —Principle-Centered Leadership

If this Skilltrack Leadership Publication is helpful to you as you do your own learning, we have fulfilled our mission. The following topics intend to give some guidance in your self-directed development journey: from a library experience toward leadership excellence in Christian ministry.

1. **Why Leadership Development?** There are many good reasons why a Christian ministry leader would want consistently to pursue improvement and development. Why?—because of the benefits of leadership development to you personally, to your family members, to your ministry performance, to your congregation, and to your community. We believe that SkillTrack® Leadership has been making a contribution to these benefits, and that Servant Leaders Today Web site and Library will expand the benefits to many others. So, let's explore further the "why" of development:

    - **Survival**—avoid termination: survival in the workplace may not be an unworthy, if only basic, motive for staying effective in your work.

    - **Stability**—enjoy tenure: stay in a place of ministry over a period of time so that you enlarge your contribution of service.

    - **Effectiveness**—competent ministry: there is a sense of professional well-being when you do your several tasks consistently well.

    - **Stewardship**—larger service: if you are "faithful over a few things," you will be prepared for larger responsibilities.

    - **Satisfaction**—making a difference: great satisfaction comes with contributing to the spiritual health of a congregation, its members, and the wider community.

↬ **Fulfillment**—a final reward: nothing is more motivating than to hear from our Lord His own approval, *"Well done, good and faithful servant! You have been faithful with a few things; I will put you in charge of many things."* (Matt.25:23 NIV)

2. **Why Development?—To Lead Congregational Mission and Functions**

Ministry leaders have the significant responsibility to shape and lead the mission and functions of the congregation. At least ten such functions require the continuous and life-time development of leadership skills and practices. Six of these are often considered "biblical functions" (marked by *); the other four may be necessary to implement the six, to bring to wholeness the life and work of the congregation.

↬ Congregational worship*

↬ Education/discipleship*

↬ Spiritual disciplines

↬ Prayer ministry*

↬ Evangelism/witnessing*

↬ Church growth and health

↬ Ministry/service*

↬ Loving/caring fellowship*

↬ Mission participation

↬ Leadership/administration

3. **Leadership Development—Why Are You in the Picture?**

Throughout society and its workforce, there is an expectation, if not requirement, that employees stay up in their professional work. The "why" of continual improvement is quite often explained to that workforce. Why should not excellence be expected of those of us who labor in the eternal work of Christ, "to show ourselves approved?" Among Christian ministers, who are those most likely to pursue leadership development? Our findings include those:

↬ who have assessed ministry skills and found themselves wanting;

↬ who desire to be more effective Christian leaders;

↬ who want to be a worthy example to other servant leaders;

- who are convinced that leadership can be learned;

- who open up to new ideas, concepts, and methods;

- who are willing to participate in skill development;

- who commit themselves to practice servant leadership.

These same folks may see leadership development as a fabric made up of a life-time of preparation, such as: family and early schooling; practical experiences (the "University of Hard Knocks"); college or university; seminary or divinity school; independent study and reflection; peer-group or mentoring; continuing professional education; and ministry leadership certification. Included in several of these development strategies are electronic print resources such as www.servantleaderstoday.com, and SkillTrack® Leadership Publications.

4. **Three Contemporary Leadership Development Challenges**

My assessment of the challenges facing us has emerged over the last several years of working with ministers, churches, and others who help with leadership training. We have much work to do in all three challenge areas that are identified:

- **"What is the #1 challenge** for comprehensive ministry leadership training?" *For pastors, staff members, and lay leaders to value, pursue, practice, and take responsibility for life-long leadership development.*

- **"What is the #2 challenge** for comprehensive ministry leadership training?" *For congregations to value, expect, support, provide for, and reward life-long leadership development.*

- **"What is the #3 challenge** for comprehensive ministry leadership training?" *For an expanding Christian network to make available development resources: basic and innovative; biblical and practical; specialized and comprehensive; flexible and affordable for all leaders in ministry.*

5. **How? Five Approaches to Leadership Development**

The Servant Leaders Library could contribute to many of the approaches to leadership development including, for example, the following five:

- **As-Needed Application**: seek specific training when it is needed to perform an immediate leadership task. *"I need to learn how to improve my delegation skill in order for every member of our evangelism team to contribute to our assignment."* **Action**: choose two or three Library articles on delegation, study them carefully, and write a specific action plan for effective delegation to achieve the task.

- ✍ **Designed Development**: keep in mind knowledge and skills that are needed in the on-going performance of a major function in your ministry role (short-time effort for long-term benefit). *"For the next three months I am going to learn by specific study, practice, and reflection the skills of interpersonal communication, especially with church members and small groups."* **Action**: choose a series of free Library articles and study them carefully, take notes about crucial insights, practice every day, talk it over with others, seek feedback, outline your plan, and evaluate your progress.

- ✍ **Life-Long Journey**: build your leadership development directly on your several tasks and expectations. *"Because I want to pursue excellence in Christian ministry, I will explore resources and tools as a life-long student of servant leadership and skills for my life and ministry."* **Action**: build the development plan on your present position description, but also on the direction you want to go; stay ahead, go beyond what others expect, both in content and method; use this Library and SkillTrack® Leadership curriculum; pursue CEU's, certification programs, ministry peer-groups, reading, viewing, and listening programs, sabbatical studies, etc.

- ✍ **Learn in Order to Teach**: all along the way apply your study and development toward the growth and enrichment of others. *"I must learn, apply, and develop others in their concepts and skills for ministry leadership."* **Action**: teaching and training are the staple of most ministry assignments, but to make it happen you must become intentional and consistent; serve as instructor, coach, and mentor; utilize this SLT Library and SkillTrack® Leadership and expand your stream of resources; research, write, and publish.

- ✍ **Academic Studies**: you may choose to enroll or continue in academic programs of ministry expansion and development. *"I will enroll in seminary and complete a masters degree in 'Pastoral Ministry and Leadership' for a life of congregational servant leadership."* **Action**: begin preparation for this track by diligent study and upper-level grades in high school and college; choose wisely the seminary by seeking wise mentors and guidance; stay active in ministry experiences in local congregations and communities; apply academic study to service and leadership as you go along, not at the end of the degree. Servant Leaders Library and SkillTrack® Leadership both expand and focus on servant leadership and its skills.

6. **How? Development and the ServantLeadersToday.com Library**

Skill development practices in the midst of Christian ministry form a stream of experience that may be explored, expanded, and described for establishing models to learn leadership. This free Library is passive; it may be of passing interest or simply be ignored. But for students and ministers of all sorts—the desperate, the curious, the searching, the growing—the Library may contribute to the phases of self-motivated adult learning, skill development, and servant leadership in Christian ministry. These phases may be experienced either in sequences or in actual practice, as a cluster:

- Phase 1. Assessment: initial condition—Why do I need to learn this leadership skill?

- Phase 2. Cognitive: explore a concept or skill until a mental image is formed; instruction is one of the roles of this free Library.

- Phase 3. Association: associate the mental image of the skill being learned to knowledge already experienced and understood.

- Phase 4. Perception: the interpretation of the information now being received becomes yours; you understand and "own" it.

- Phase 5. Demonstration: act on the new information; listen, watch, do, and try again.

- Phase 6. Repetition: the action or behavior is repeated, and concept is tested.

- Phase 7. Reflection: the performance and results will be assessed; feedback and consensus are measured and merged into the learning cycle.

Conclusion: Why develop as a servant leader? Exploring the Library may move you along other paths of your growth as a servant leader in the ministry of Christ. These topics offer at least some beginning answers to the question "Why and How?" for developing proven skills and best practices.

ANNOTATED BIBLIOGRAPHY
Time and Stress Management

Bibliography, References and Study Resources: Published and Internet

T he annotated bibliography has two major functions: to provide full information for citations throughout this book; and, to serve as study resources for those wishing to continue their own research. Annotations, prepared primarily by Lloyd Elder, seek to support both functions. The bibliography is arranged for focus:

    A. Recognition for Zondervan Biblical Study References

    B. Internet Resources: General Study and Time Management

    C. Time and Time Management: Book Resources

    D. Stress and Stress Management Resources: Books and Internet Links

A. Recognition for Biblical Study References – Zondervan Publishing House

More than a decade ago, **Zondervan Publishing House** granted permission for the Moench Center and Skilltrack Leadership to use their electronic library in authoring study material for ministry leadership training. Although in this publication we have reduced our dependence to normal copyright standards, the author wishes to express grateful appreciation to Zondervan, and to acknowledge all rights reserved as publisher. Specifically noted:

"The NIV Study Bible Basic Library"—published by Zondervan Publishing House (www.zondervan.com) products in both book and CD-ROM format

"The Expositor's Bible Commentary"—published by Zondervan Publishing House (www.zondervan.com) products in both book and CD-ROM format

"New International Dictionary of New Testament Theology"—published by Zondervan Publishing House (www.zondervan.com) products in both book and CD-ROM format

B. Internet Resources: General Study and Time Management

Selections for Time Management, Biblical Study, Ministry, and Leadership; also, by navigating the Website menus, find **time, stress, leadership, management**, and related topics.

Alban Institute: http://www.alban.org/ —a ministry resource site with changing options

Art and Science of Leadership —www.nwlink.com/~donclark/leader/leader.html

Bible Gateway—http://bible.gospelcom.net

Bible Studies Foundation—http://www.bible.org

Christian Leadership World: http://www.teal.org.uk/index.htm—*Brief topical papers, many supporting ministry and servant leadership*

Crosswalk.com Bible Study Tools—http://bible.crosswalk.com

Dictionary.com—http://www.dictionary.com—search related topics, time, stress, etc.

Free Management Library—http://www.mapnp.org/library—*An extensive, valuable library of leadership theories, practice, and skills; for serious students!*

Greenleaf Center for Servant Leadership—http://www.greenleaf.org—*This center is a leader in the modern movement of servant leadership, not only in non-profit organizations, but also in education and commerce.*

Institute for Business Technology: "Personal Efficiency Program"—www.ibt-pep.com—*See especially IBT Tips (menu) for five articles related to time management; it also promotes Gleeson's Personal Efficiency Program.*

Leader to Leader Institute—http:/www.drucker.com

Leadership Links—http://www.tmcenter.lmi.net/pages/

Management Center Links Library—http://www.tmcenter.org/pages

Moench Center for Church Leadership—http://www.belmont.edu/moench—See also SkillTrack® Leadership *Provides SkillTrack Leadership curriculum for ministry leadership training.*

SkillTrack® Leadership—www.servantleaderstoday.com/—This site is hosted by SkillTrack® Leadership providing free leadership training materials and educational curriculum at scholarship prices.

SmallChurch.com—http://www.smallchurch.com/rprisk.htm —Search *stress* and *risk*; time management, *several sources as "Risk Factors for Pastors."*

PACE Productivity: "Time Tips"—http://www.getmoredone.com/tips5.html—*A series of excellent articles that would provide for advanced study in areas of time use.*

Preacher's Study: "General Areas Where a Minister Spends Time" http://preacherstudy. com/time2.html—*Enriches the topics of ministry tasks, but contributes ideas and suggestions toward other time-use strategies.*

Sonic.net: "Guide to Better Time Management"—http://www.sonic.net/~infreeman/time-hlp.htm—*Excellent articles covering ten valuable tips for effective time management.*

YourDictionary.com—http://www.yourdictionary.com

C. Time and Time Management: Book Resources

Alexander, Roy. Commonsense Time Management. New York: American Management Association, 1992. *A broad look at issues relating to time management. There are many tips, techniques, and warnings about time-wasters.*

Axelrod, Alan and Jim Holtje. 201 Ways To Manage Your Time Better. New York, NY: McGraw-Hill, 1997. *These 201 ways organized into over 20 categories, serve as "a quick-tip survival guide" to better time management. The book is practical and a master at thumbnail sketches.*

Bittle, Lester R. and John W. Newstrom. What Every Supervisor Should Know, 6th edition. New York, NY: McGraw-Hill, 1990. (See pp. 525-558 of this developmental book.) *This excellent treatment of managing job-related time is in the larger context of part 8, "Personal Development Portfolio."*

Bruce, Andy and Ken Langdon. <u>Do It Now!</u> New York, NY: DK Publishing, Inc., 2001. *In the DK Essential Managers Series, this 72-page book focuses primarily on work-setting issues such as organizing, prioritizing, balancing, assessing, deadlines, etc.*

Cook, Marshall J. <u>Time Management: Proven Techniques for Making the Most of Your Valuable Time</u>. Madison, WI: Adams Media Corporation, 1998. *The twelve-page detailed outline of this 229-page book presents a challenging action plan for you if you want to accept the challenge for making the most of your valuable time.*

Covey, Stephen R. <u>First Things First: a Fireside Book</u>. Simon and Schuster, 1994. *Covey sets time management inside the context of living and working from a life-compass, not simply a clock.*

Daytimer®-<u>Solutions for Success</u>: "Time Power for Today;" Day-Timers, Inc., 1996. *A one-hour entertaining and educational video promising to help discover how to get the most from your "Day-Timer Personal Organizer."*

Elder, Lloyd. <u>Time Management: Having the Time of Your Life</u> (CD-ROM Course and Study Guide format) Nashville, Tennessee: Published by SkillTrack® Leadership and the Moench Center for Church Leadership, Belmont University, 2001—2006. As a *distance education/interactive course on time management, this SkillTrack study has been used effectively for training Christian ministers and ministry teams. That continuing practical experience has also become a primary recourse for this published work.*

Gleeson, Kerry. <u>The Personal Efficiency Program; How to Get Organized To Do More Work In Less Time</u>, (2nd ed.) New York, NY: John Wiley & Sons, Inc., 2000. *Gleeson claims the "missing link," supplied by his Personal Efficiency Program) is that in the white collar world there is a lack of knowledge of how to process personal work to achieve both quality of life and quantity of productivity. Much of his program relates to time-use.*

Grenz, Arlo. <u>The Confident Leader</u>. Nashville: Broadman and Holman, 1994. *Chapter 15 is an excellent, brief treatment of a minister's time management under the heading, "All in Good Time."*

Harvard Business School Press. "Harvard Business Review on Work and Life Balance." Boston, MA: Harvard Business School Press, 2000. *Though not a book specifically on time management, this collection of articles probes into issues contributing to a balanced life, for men and women.*

Hindle, Tim. <u>Manage Your Time. New York</u>: DK Publishing, 1998. *A book from the Essential Managers series of brief works on leadership topics. This volume, like the*

others, is packed full of practical solutions, visual aids, clear and concise modules on each sub-topic.

Jenson, Dr. Ron. <u>Make a Life, Not Just a Living</u>. Nashville: Broadman & Holman, 1998. *Dr. Jenson offers 10 "timeless skills" to help you re-define your view of "success." Leading a balanced, fulfilled life is the ultimate goal.*

Lakein, Alan. <u>How To Get Control of Your Time and Your Life</u>. New York: Signet Books, 1973. *This somewhat older book emphasizes the importance of gaining freedom in your life due to better time management. Some important contemporary ideas are not included, e.g., the need for delegation and team-building, the importance of empowering those around you, etc.*

McCarty, Doran C. <u>Making the Most of Your Time</u>. The McCarty Library, 1996. *This concise booklet is designed particularly for bivocational ministers. A great resource for those who need brief, effective, practical tips for managing a minister's time.*

McGee-Cooper, Ann, with Duane Trammell. <u>Time Management for Unmanageable People</u>. New York: Bantam Books, 1994. *This book of 250 pages for very busy people in a hectic business world could benefit 21st-century Christian ministers. It is inspiring, enjoyable, creative, and practical; it could lead toward balance in your life.*

Morgenstern, Jule. <u>Time Management from the Inside Out</u>. New York, NY: Henry Holt and Company, LLC, 2000. *The books' subtitle, "The Foolproof System for Taking Control of Your Schedule—and Your Life" proposes that time management for you should be about designing a schedule that is a custom fit for you. It's about identifying your personality needs and goals and scheduling to bring you a feeling of satisfaction at the end of each day.*

Newcombe, Jerry & Kirsti. <u>I'll Do it Tomorrow: How to Stop Putting it Off and Get It Done Today</u>. Nashville: Broadman & Holman, 1999. *A collaboration between the authors and popular comic strip cartoonist, Johnny Hart (B.C., The Wizard of Id), this book deals with procrastination in a humorous and helpful way. The Newcombes communicate through personal anecdote, story-telling and plain good advice.*

Sherman, Doug and Hendricks, William. <u>How to Balance Competing Time Demands</u>. Colorado Springs: Navpress, 1989. *Balance is the organizing concept of a "Pentathlon" of life: personal life, family life, work, church, and community. Very helpful and practical.*

Short, Mark. <u>Time Management for Ministers</u>. Nashville: Broadman Press, 1987. *A book in the "Broadman Leadership Series," this book is brief, clear, focused, and practical* in the several areas related to time management. It includes chapters on scheduling, delegating, decision-making, effective meetings, and planning for leisure.

Smith, Hyrum W. <u>The 10 Natural Laws of Successful Time and Life Management: Proven Strategies for Increased Productivity and Inner Peace</u>. New York: Warner Books, 1994. *Part I of this book on "Managing Your Time" is most directly related to the topic here, but the entire work is focused on using your time to change your whole life for the better. Controlling your time and controlling your life, he says, are dependent upon each other.*

D. Stress and Stress Management Resources: Internet Links and Books

The following links are provided for specific resources on *"stress"* **and** *"stress management."* For the following links, check the home page content or index to find references related to "stress management." In addition, for your own internet search on "stress," "stress management," or "eustress," use Google or other search engines and review articles. We have found the following to have useful resources:

Stress Management Internet Links Resources

American Institute of Stress: <u>http://www.stress.org/</u>—search *stress and burnout for excellent help.*

Dictionary.com: <u>http://www.dictionary.com</u> —For helpful dictionary and thesaurus entries search on any key word, such as: <u>stress</u>, <u>stress management</u>, <u>anxiety</u>, <u>burnout</u>, <u>attitude</u>, <u>eustress</u>, <u>stage fright</u>, <u>behavior</u>, etc.

Health Education: <u>http://www.teachhealth.com/</u>—Search *stress on this site*

John Hopkins University: <u>http://www.jhu.edu/</u> —Search *stress* and *eustress*

LearnWell Institute, Managing Stress: <u>http://www.learnwell.org/stress.htm</u>

Mental Help.net: Stress Reduction and Management—*an extensive research source:* <u>http://www.mentalhelp.net/poc/center_index.php?id=117&cn=117</u>

Mind Tools: Stress: <u>http://www.mindtools.com</u>—Search *stress*

Stress and Emotional Wellness Links: <u>http://www.optimalhealthconcepts.com/Stress</u>—*links and resources are provided on "The Web's Stress Management & Emotional Wellness Page"*

Stress Management—Oklahoma State University: http://ehs.okstate.edu/links/stress.htm—numerous *resources for the study of stress management and stress related resources*

Stress Management Sites: http://www.helpself.com/directory/stress.htm—*the ABC's of Self Help, providing an extensive listing of resources on stress, anxiety, and related topics.*

Stress Management Society—http://www.stress.org.uk/—*presents stress, its causes, symptoms, solution, and benefits*

Symptoms of Anxiety: Archibald Hart—http://www.troubledwith.com/—search *life pressures, anxiety, stress*

Stress Management Book Resources

Allen, David. Getting Things Done: The Art of Stress-Free Productivity. New York: Penguin Books, 2001.—*A relaxed, clear mind is the key to increased productivity with less harmful stress, according to Allen in this insightful book.*

Benson, Herbert, M.D. and Eileen M. Stuart, R.N., M.S., editors. The Wellness Book: The Comprehensive Guide to Maintaining Health and Stress-Related Illness. New York: A Fireside book published by Simon & Schuster, 1992.—*this book lives up to its title; worth serious research and application.*

Chandler, Charles. Minister's Support Group: Alternative to Burnout. Nashville, TN: Convention Press, 1987.—*the pros and cons, the why's and how's, of setting up or joining a minister's support group to help manage stress.*

Charlesworth, Edward A. and Ronald G. Nathan. Stress Management: A Comprehensive Guide to Wellness. New York: Ballantine Books, 1984.—*Focuses on our need to fight stresses that threaten our body's wellness; an introductory, thorough guide.*

Davidson, Jeff. The Complete Idiot's Guide to Managing Stress. Indianapolis, IN: Alpha Books, 1999.—*Despite its title in a series, this is a thorough and easy-to-read introduction to stress and stress management.*

Ecker, Richard E. The Stress Myth. Downers Grove, IL: Intervarsity Press, 1985.—*Dr. Ecker outlines a "preventionist" approach to stress management, as opposed to the predominant "interventionist" way of thinking.*

Elder, Lloyd. SkillTrack® Vol. 11, Stress Management: Getting on Top of Stress in Ministry. (2nd Ed.) SkillTrack Leadership and the Moench Center for Church Leadership, 1998—

2005. *A text/workbook on stress in ministry and in life, from the SkillTrack®Leadership series on church leadership. It is a substantial source, along with the practical research in seminars and conferences, for this work now being published.*

Girdano, Daniel A.; Everly, Jr., G. S.; and Duseck, Dorothy E. <u>Controlling Stress and Tension</u> (6th ed.). Needham Heights, MA: Allyn & Bacon, 2001. — *A comprehensive look at the physiological side of excess stress, proposing the need of living in harmony within society.*

Faulkner, Brooks, (compiler). <u>Stress in the Life of the Minister</u>. Nashville, TN: Convention Press, 1981. — *Faulkner brings together a series of essays on stress challenges faced by ministers, both in personal and professional life.*

Harris, John C. <u>Stress, Power and Ministry</u>. Washington D.C. The Alban Institute, 1977. — *Though dated, this is a tough-minded and personal discussion of the related issues of stress and power affecting the ministry.*

Hawkins, O. S. <u>High Calling/High Stress: Advice from James for Managing Stress in Ministry</u>. Dallas, TX. Annuity Board (Guidestone), 2003. — *a series of practical sermons applied to those in ministry.*

Loehr, James E. <u>Stress for Success</u>. New York, NY: Three Rivers Press, 1997. — *A 30-day program that tries to prepare you physically, mentally and emotionally for stress, by teaching you to feed off of its energy in a positive way.*

McCarty, Doran C. <u>Making the Most of Coping with Anxiety, Stress, Burnout</u>. The McCarty Library, 2000. — *this brief text is a fine biblical and practical treatment of "stress;" it is in The McCarty Library for "developing leaders for a demanding age."*

Miles, Mary Dell. <u>Stress</u>. Nashville, TN: Abingdon Press, 1994. — *designed for small-group discussions, this text and workbook on stress is a part of the LifeSearch series.*

Parker, Gary. <u>Creative Tensions: Personal Growth Through Stress</u>. Nashville, TN: Broadman Press, 1991. — *this text explores the opportunities to turn stress into positive challenges and growth in your life.*

Porowski, James P. and Paul B. Carlisle. <u>Strength for the Journey: A Biblical Perspective on Discouragement and Depression</u>. Nashville, TN: LifeWay Press, 1999. — *intensely biblical study in nine units designed for personal and small-group reflection and discussion; includes daily assignments.*

Sheehan, David V., M.D. <u>The Anxiety Disease: New Medical Breakthroughs</u>. New York: Bantam Books, 1983, 1990.—*promises new hope for the millions who suffer from anxiety.*

Swenson, Richard A., M.D. <u>Margin: Restoring Emotional, Physical, Financial, and Time Reserves to Overloaded Lives</u>. Colorado Springs, CO: NavPress, 1992.—*Dr. Swenson believes stress is rampant because we live without margins today. This text is an attempt to revitalize "that space that once existed between ourselves and our limits."*

Wellness Center Newsletter. C. L., Mee, Jr., et al. Nashville Fall, 1995. — *Belmont University. reproduced from* <u>Managing Stress from Morning to Night</u>. *Alexandria, VA: Time-Life Books, 1987, p. 27.*

Whiteman, Dr. Thomas, Verghese, Dr. Sam, and Randy Petersen. <u>The Complete Stress Management Workbook: Your Personal Step-by-Step Program for Handling the Stress in Your Life</u>. Grand Rapids, MI: Zondervan Publishing, 1996.—*A comprehensive introduction to issues of stress and stress management.*

Younger, Brett; and Younger, Carol. <u>Living With Stress: Nurturing Joy in a Tension-Filled World</u>. Macon, GA, Smyth & Helwys Publishing, 1994.—*divided into five study sessions providing interactive teaching options.*

CPSIA information can be obtained at www.ICGtesting.com
Printed in the USA
LVOW110213070513

332408LV00001B/2/P